New Ways to Enjoy CHICKEN

Stanley Wolf

A Special Collection of Quick and Easy Everyday Recipes

REVISED EDITION

A Nitty Gritty₍ Cookbook

Printed in the United States of America.

ISBN 1-55867-001-7

Designed by Mike Nelson
Edited by Jackie Walsh
Photographs by Glen Millward
Food Stylist: Bobbie Greenlaw

TABLE OF CONTENTS

METRIC CONVERSION CHART

Liquid or Dry Measuring Cup (based on an 8 ounce cup)
1/4 cup = 60 ml
1/3 cup = 80 ml
1/2 cup = 125 ml
3/4 cup = 190 ml
1 cup = 250 ml
2 cups = 500 ml

Liquid or Dry Measuring Cup (based on a 10 ounce cup)
1/4 cup = 80 ml
1/3 cup = 100 ml
1/2 cup = 150 ml
3/4 cup = 230 ml
1 cup = 300 ml
2 cups = 600 ml

Liquid or Dry Teaspoon and Tablespoon
1/4 tsp. = 1.5 ml
1/2 tsp. = 3 ml
1 tsp. = 5 ml
3 tsp. = 1 tbs. = 15 ml

Temperatures

°F		°C
200	=	100
250	=	120
275	=	140
300	=	150
325	=	160
350	=	180
375	=	190
400	=	200
425	=	220
450	=	230
475	=	240
500	=	260
550	=	280

Pan Sizes (1 inch = 25mm)
8-inch pan (round or square) = 200 mm x 200 mm
9-inch pan (round or square) = 225 mm x 225 mm
9 x 5 x 3-inch loaf pan = 225 mm x 125 mm x 75 mm
1/4 inch thickness = 5 mm
1/8 inch thickness = 2.5 mm

Pressure Cooker
100 Kpa = 15 pounds per square inch
70 Kpa = 10 pounds per square inch
35 Kpa = 5 pounds per square inch

Mass
1 ounce = 30 g
4 ounces = 1/4 pound = 125 g
8 ounces = 1/2 pounds = 250 g
16 ounces = 1 pound = 500 g
2 pounds = 1 kg

Key   (America uses an 8 ounce cup — Britain uses a 10 ounce cup)

ml = milliliter
l = liter
g = gram
K = Kilo (one thousand)
mm = millimeter
m = mill (a thousandth)
°F = degrees Fahrenheit

°C = degrees Celsius
tsp. = teaspoon
tbs. = tablespoon
Kpa = (pounds pressure per square inch)
      This configuration is used for pressure cookers only.

Metric equivalents are rounded to conform to existing metric measuring utensils.

INTRODUCTION

Present day chickens are descended from the jungle of Southeast Asia and appear to have been domesticated as early as 2500 B.C. However, until recent times, they remained an infrequent luxury at the dinner table. It used to take months to raise a bird to maturity, and hens were prized for their egg producing capability. As a result, the chickens which were picked for consumption were either stringy roasters or tough, old hens. Tender, young fowl were rarely available, and considered a special delicacy.

Today, of course, the situation has dramatically improved. Chicken is widely available and at very reasonable prices. Tender, young birds, (known as broilers or fryers) are no longer a rarity. Instead they are the variety which is most commonly marketed. This rapid change in the availability and quality of chickens has been due to the ingenuity of American poultry farmers and agricultural researchers. They worked to develop special breeding and nourishing techniques for producing plump and juicy chickens. They perfected methods which reduced the time required to mature the birds from months, to just weeks. Finally, they promoted efficient processing procedures and the use of rapid, refrigerated transportation to insure the delivery of fresh poultry to market. Thanks to this progress, chickens are now enjoyed regularly as a part of our diet.

Chicken is one of our favorite foods. We Americans enjoy its taste, appreciate its economy, and rely on its nutritional value. But the fact that chicken is also an extraordinarily versatile food is not as well recognized. Few cooks are aware that chicken is capable of being prepared in a greater number of ways than any other type of meat or fish. All too often, family chicken dinners are limited to fried chicken, or some type of chicken stew. Unfortunately, if a dish is served too frequently, some of its appeal is apt to be lost. Thus, the low-cost and nutritional benefits of chicken are not fully realized.

The inspiration for writing this book sprang from a desire to present a collection of recipes which would focus on the special versatility of chicken. The idea was to provide a source containing a wide variety of new and interesting ways to prepare chicken. It was hoped that many cooks would use it to learn to prepare and serve this economical and popular fowl more regularly. With this goal in mind, the book has been organized in the following manner: Some chapters include recipes in which only a specific cooking technique is utilized, such as roasting or barbecuing. Other chapters are dedicated to a particular category of ingredients with which chicken can be prepared, fruits, nuts, and spirits are some examples. Finally, some chapters are reserved for collections of more exotic recipes; these include international and oriental classics. Most traditional favorites have also been presented. Readers will also notice that recipes have been picked with an eye toward ease of preparation and minimum cooking time. Thus, the busy cook will discover many selections that are delicious, yet quick and easy to prepare. More elaborate meals for company or that special occasion have not been neglected. There are many choices which will certainly dazzle even the most discriminating of food-lovers. All in all, it is hoped that the book will provide creative cooks with a vehicle for uncovering new and delightful chicken surprises.

CHICKEN WISDOM
WHAT'S SO GREAT ABOUT CHICKEN?

Everything! Most important of all, chicken is really good for you. It's delicious and it's one of today's best food values. Chicken is an excellent source of high-quality protein, a fine source of niacin, riboflavin, calcium, Vitamin A and minerals. It is lower in fat and calories than most other meats and it is easy to digest.

LIGHT MEAT 3-1/2 ounces, without skin = 166 calories
DARK MEAT 3-1/2 ounces, without skin = 176 calories

Chicken is so versatile you can serve it often and still not run out of interesting ways to prepare it. If you are cutting down on red meat in your diet and want to serve chicken several times a week, it is important to have variety in the way it's prepared. For instance, serve broiled chicken for one meal, a new recipe from this collection of favorites for another, and fried chicken for Saturday night's supper. If your family is small, roast chicken is a perfect choice because there will be leftovers for delicious sandwiches or perhaps a casserole or chicken salad.

Enjoy the economy and nutritional benefits of chicken often. The basic information on the next few pages will be extremely helpful in its selection and preparation.

BE AN EXPERT WHEN BUYING CHICKEN

The most reliable rule for purchasing chicken is: the fresher the better. Fresh chickens which have never been frozen are preferable over frozen ones, but a properly cared for frozen chicken can be delicious, too. The important thing regarding a frozen chicken is to be sure it has not been stored too long, that its wrapping is still intact to prevent freezer burn and that it has never been partially defrosted. When you buy a frozen chicken, inspect it thoroughly for signs of freezer burn or evidence of having been refrozen. Pinkish-colored ice in the package is a sign that the chicken has been at least partially defrosted and refrozen. A chicken that has been refrozen will be tough and lacking in flavor.

Chickens are marketed under several different names, depending upon their age and weight. The following are the most commonly used classifications:

Broilers and Fryers: weigh from 2 to 4 pounds and are from 7 to 9 weeks old. They are bred for maximum tenderness. Broilers and fryers can be sauteed, roasted, broiled, fried or grilled.

Roasting Chickens: weigh from 3 to 5 pounds. They are slightly older than broilers and fryers, therefore a little less tender.

Capons: weigh from 4 to 8 pounds. They are roosters which have been castrated to improve their flavor and plumpness. Although older than roasting chickens, they are more tender.

Stewing Chickens: weigh from 4 to 7 pounds. They are the oldest of the four main types of chickens described here. Their flesh is tougher but rich in flavor. They are suitable for stewing only.

Chicken Parts: can be purchased separately. Packages of legs, thighs, breasts (boned and unboned), wings and backs can be found at your local market.

Chicken Giblets: the gizzard, heart and liver of the chicken can be found either inside a whole chicken or packaged separately.

GUIDELINES FOR STORING CHICKEN

Chicken can be stored in the refrigerator or freezer according to the following guidelines:

Refrigerator Shelf:
Raw: Should be kept no longer than 2 days. Make sure to keep it well covered with plastic wrap to prevent drying out, but loose enough for air to circulate around chicken.

Cooked: Will keep well for no longer than a week. Make sure to keep it well covered.

Refrigerator Freezing Compartment:
Raw: Will keep for up to 2 months, if packaged in an airtight container, or tightly wrapped and sealed in freezer paper.

Cooked: Will keep for 2 weeks, if packaged in an airtight container, plastic wrap or freezer paper.

Freezer (0°F.):
　　Raw:　　　　Will keep for up to 6 months, if packaged in an
　　　　　　　　airtight container or freezer paper.
　　Cooked:　　Will keep for up to 1 month, if packaged in an
　　　　　　　　airtight container.

Once a chicken is defrosted, do not refreeze it. Use it within 2 days of thawing. If the thawing is done on a refrigerator shelf, allow 3 to 4 hours thawing time per pound. For example, a 2 to 3 pound broiler/fryer should thaw in 8 to 12 hours. To thaw more rapidly, place wrapped chicken in a pan under running water. Allow 1/2 to 1 hour per pound for broiler/fryers using this method. A microwave oven can thaw a frozen bird even more rapidly. Follow the directions in your microwave oven instruction book. To guarantee even cooking throughout, make sure a chicken is thoroughly defrosted prior to cooking.

FIVE EASY STEPS FOR CUTTING UP A CHICKEN

AN IMPORTANT FACT TO REMEMBER: It is much less expensive to buy a whole chicken and disjoint it yourself, than it is to buy separately packaged chicken parts. By learning how to cut chicken into pieces, you not only save money, but will end up with neater looking portions once you learn how it's done. It is really quite easy if you possess a sharp knife, a cutting board and a familiarity with the technique. For step-by-step instruction, with drawings, read the following:

1. TO REMOVE LEGS:
Place chicken on its back on a cutting board. Pull one leg away from the body and cut through the skin all the way down to the joint. Lift the chicken and bend the leg back until the thighbone is separated from the body. Repeat on other leg.

2. TO DIVIDE LEGS FROM THIGHS:

Grasp the drumstick in one hand and the thigh in the other. By bending the leg and thigh together, towards the center and the joint, you'll be able to locate the knee joint. Cut through this joint.

3. TO REMOVE WING FROM BODY:

Locate wing joint by rotating wing slightly. Cut on the inside of the wing, through the joint. Remove as little of the breast meat as possible. Repeat with other wing.

4. DIVIDING BREAST AND BACK:

Stand chicken on its neck and cut down along the breast end of the rib bones on each side. Separate the breast and back. Divide back into two pieces by breaking it at the joint and cutting through.

5. TO HALVE BREAST:

Place breast on cutting board, skin side up. Cut down along entire length of breastbone to separate breast into two halves.

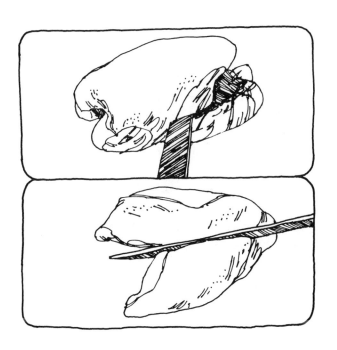

11

BONING A CHICKEN BREAST

Boning chicken breasts yourself serves two useful purposes. First, if chicken breasts are purchased already boned, they will have begun to lose some of their moisture and delightful flavor. Boning just prior to cooking helps to create a more delicious dish. Second, already boned breasts are relatively expensive. However, by boning breasts at home, chicken breast recipes become quite economical.

By the way, a chicken has only a single breast. That is, the entire portion of the chest, from the neck to the belly, is known as the breast of the chicken (including the skin, flesh and bones). The breast is usually halved after boning. Each half contains two filets, one slightly larger than the other. A boned, skinless breast half is also known as a supreme. The supreme is considered to be the finest part of the bird. If you have had the good fortune to savor perfectly prepared supremes, you will wholeheartedly agree.

How To Debone a Chicken Breast

1. Remove the skin from the breast by grasping the skin firmly in one hand and the flesh and bone in the other. Pull firmly to separate.

2. Place breast, skinned side down on a cutting board. Slit the thin membrane that covers the breastbone.

3. Grasp the breast and bend the breastbone at the wide end to separate it from the collarbones.

13

4. Twist the breastbone at the narrow end of the breast to separate it from the cartilage.

5. Gently pry out breastbone. Remove ribs by lifting them with your fingers.

6. Cut away cartilage from narrow end of breast. Carefully remove collarbones using the tip of a knife to cut through the flesh.

7. Using the tip of a knife, make a small incision along the length of the wishbone. Work the bone free with your fingers. Pull it out. It may be necessary to cut the flesh from the ends of the wishbone to take it out.

8. Cut the breast in half lengthwise to yield two supremes.

CHICKEN MAGIC
EASY BASIC WAYS TO COOK CHICKEN

Chicken is extraordinarily versatile. It can be prepared in a greater number of ways than any other type of meat or fish.

Two of the most basic and useful methods of cooking chicken are **sauteing** and **braising**. Many recipes call for one or the other as a preliminary step. Once you have become familiar with each of these methods cooking chicken will become even simpler. The other popular ways of cooking chicken are **roasting, broiling, barbecuing** and **frying.** They are each briefly described on the next few pages. More explicit directions are given later in the book.

Sauteing: is a method of pan frying chicken which uses just enough fat to keep the flesh from adhering to the bottom of the skillet. The chicken pieces are cooked over high heat, so that the surface of the chicken will become seared and golden brown. Sauteing works particularly well for young broiler and fryer chickens that have been cut into pieces.

A lot of recipes call for sauteing chicken just until it's brown. To do this, follow

How to Saute Chicken, step 1. If you want to completely cook your chicken, follow How to Saute Chicken, steps 1 and 2.

How to Saute Chicken

Step 1: Pat chicken pieces dry with a paper towel. It's important to remove any surface moisture, because it will inhibit the browning process. Place a small amount of fat in a skillet (about 2 tablespoons for a 10-inch skillet), and heat it to a high temperature. Place chicken pieces in skillet and cook until golden brown on all sides. This will take about 6 minutes. Use tongs to turn chicken pieces. Never use a fork, or a sharp instrument since they pierce the flesh and allow the juices which keep the chicken moist to escape.

Step 2: Follow step 1. Reduce the heat to medium-low and cover the skillet. Continue cooking the chicken, about 15 minutes for white meat and 20 minutes for dark meat. Turn pieces occasionally with tongs during cooking process.

Braising: is a method of cooking chicken in which the chicken (whole or in pieces) is first sauteed until brown (follow step 1 of How to Saute Chicken). Then simmered until done in a liquid that partially covers it. Cooking may take place in a skillet or a casserole. Vegetables, herbs and spices are generally added to the liquid in which the chicken cooks. Fats rise to the top of the skillet or casserole as the chicken cooks. They should be skimmed off and discarded before serving.

Braising can be successfully applied to the cooking of broilers and fryers, as well as more mature birds, such as roasting chickens, capons and stewing chickens. Remember to allow more cooking time for the older birds.

When the liquid of a braised chicken dish is enriched at the end of the cooking time by the addition of eggs and cream, the result is known as a fricassee.

Roasting: chicken is cooked uncovered in an oven until the skin is richly browned and the meat is succulent and juicy. The steps to perfectly roasted chicken are outlined in the chapter entitled Roast Chicken, Modern and Marvelous, page 22.

Broiling and Barbecuing: are methods in which radiant heat is used to cook chicken quickly. In broiling and barbecuing the most moist and delicious results are achieved if intense heat causes the outside of the chicken to become browned and crisp, while allowing the natural juices of the chicken to remain sealed in. See the chapter entitled Succulent Broiled or Barbecued Chicken for more details (page 41).

Frying: is a method in which chicken is cooked in oil or fat in a skillet. There are two types of frying: pan frying, which uses small amounts of oil; and deep-fat frying, which uses large amounts of oil. The trick with both of these methods is to keep the oil hot enough to cook the chicken without burning it. If the oil isn't hot enough, the chicken will become greasy and take longer to cook. To insure that the oil stays hot, don't crowd the pan. For more details see Deep Fried Chicken (page 108).

MARINATING MAKES A DIFFERENCE

Marinating chicken adds a whole new dimension to its flavor. Subtle combinations of liquids, herbs and spices penetrate the flesh and produce exceptionally tender and juicy chicken. Acidic liquids, such as lemon juice, wine and vinegar, break down the muscle tissue of the chicken, making it more tender. Oils work to seal in the juices. Chicken is often marinated prior to broiling, barbecuing, sauteing or deep-fat frying.

To Marinate: immerse the chicken completely in the marinade. Not only will the marinade work faster, but the chicken will be more flavorful too. There are two ways of marinating chicken. You may let it stand from two to four hours at room temperature, or you may place it in the refrigerator for 24 to 48 hours. If you choose the latter method, be sure to turn the chicken twice daily. The reason for this is that the acidic liquids have a tendency to remain at the bottom. If you don't turn the chicken, it may assume a very tart and acidic flavor. After the chicken is finished marinating, dry it well with paper towels before you cook it. Leftover marinade may be used to baste the chicken while it cooks.

ELIMINATE THE GUESSWORK

Although many rule-of-thumb techniques are used to determine if a chicken has been sufficiently cooked, the only reliable and accurate method requires the insertion of an instant-registering meat thermometer into the meat. Insert the thermometer into the center of the inner thigh muscle, taking care not to make contact with the bone. Dark chicken meat is done when the internal temperature reads 180°F. and white meat is cooked when the thermometer reaches 145°F. The center of a stuffed bird should reach at least 165°F.

Other methods, such as piercing the flesh deeply and noting the color of the running juices, wiggling the drumstick, or pressing the surface and observing the resilience of the meat, are all much less dependable. It is much better to purchase an instant-registering meat thermometer and use it whenever cooking a chicken. The technique is equally accurate for all methods of cooking chicken.

Chicken Magic

ROAST CHICKEN, MODERN AND MARVELOUS

A FAMILY FAVORITE MODERNIZED

From the tantalizing aroma as it roasts to that first succulent bite, a beautifully roasted chicken is a culinary pleasure hard to beat. With my easy trussing and fast roasting method, it can be on the menu any night of the week.

Sadly, because preparing a roast chicken is thought to be a time-consuming task, it is not enjoyed as often as it should be. In reality, it is one of the easiest and best ways to prepare a chicken, and should be enjoyed often. It is nutritious, low in calories and an economical family meal.

Roasting a chicken unstuffed saves both preparation and roasting time. An unstuffed chicken can be trussed ahead of time and quickly roasted while you prepare the rest of the evening meal. Once in the oven it requires very little attention. If your family loves stuffing, it can also be made ahead and baked separately in a covered casserole.

On the following pages is a brief summary of the steps for roasting a perfect chicken just to familiarize you with the process. Don't be fooled into thinking it's difficult. Try my modernized recipe for roasting an unstuffed chicken on page 28 and see how easy and fast it really is.

(1) **Oiling or Buttering** the chicken helps seal in the juices while it's cooking and adds a fine flavor. Flavored butter can be used for variety. See recipes given on pages 34 and 35.

(2) **Stuffings**, if used, provide additional variations on the theme of the basic roast chicken. In the master recipe for Roasting a Stuffed Chicken (page 31) guidelines are presented for preparing a stuffed chicken. Several delicious stuffing recipes are given on pages 36 through 39.

(3) **Trussing** is a method of tying a chicken so that it maintains its shape while roasting. It looks more attractive and is easier to carve and handle. A simple method for trussing a chicken is shown on page 26.

(4) **Using a** rack allows heat to circulate evenly around the chicken while it roasts. Without a rack, the bottom of the bird will stew in its own juice. To start roasting, place the chicken on its side on the rack. Turning the chicken during roasting is discussed in step 7.

(5) **Timetable** giving estimated roasting times for various size birds is found on page 30. The roasting temperature of 450°F. is probably higher than those recommended in other cooking guides. Although lower temperatures can be used, 450°F. gives un-

surpassed results! The higher temperature will cause a little more spattering in the oven near the end of the roasting time, but the succulent results are worth it. If you prefer to use a lower temperature, first preheat the oven to 450°F., place the chicken in the oven and immediately reduce the temperature to 350°F.; roast the chicken for about 20 minutes per pound. Check for doneness with an instant-registering meat thermometer.

(6) **Sealing** the chicken is critical to good roasting. A one-way "screen" must be formed on the outside of the chicken which allows heat to enter, but keeps the juices from escaping. The butter or oil which is rubbed and basted onto the chicken prior to, and while roasting forms such a seal. This results in a more moist bird.

(7) **Turning** while roasting permits uniform browning and cooking of the chicken. By starting the chicken to roast while on its side and then turning periodically, the juices are evenly distributed. The chicken should be turned without piercing the skin. This can be done by inserting a fork into the neck cavity and turning the bird.

Modern Roast Chicken

EASY TRUSSING METHOD

(1) Start with a piece of clean string suitable for trussing, about 3 feet long. Place bird on its back, legs facing towards you. Tie the legs together tightly by looping the string around their ends. Try to keep the ends of string reasonably even in length. Cross the two ends of the string, pull the two ends around the tail in a loop and tighten the string. This will pull the tail up towards the legs. Bring the ends of the string along both sides of the chicken. Guide them under the drumsticks.

Modern Roast Chicken

(2) Turn chicken on its breast. Thread string through the wings and pull together along a line across the chicken back. Make sure that string is taut. Tie securely with knot, cut off any excess string.

Modern Roast Chicken

FASTER ROAST CHICKEN, UNSTUFFED

It saves last-minute time to truss an unstuffed chicken in advance. With the faster cooking time, roast chicken takes no longer than many other ways of preparing it.

1 chicken, 2-1/2 to 3 lbs.
1/2 cup butter, flavored butter or 1/3 cup oil
    (recipes for flavored butters given on pages 34 and 35)
freshly ground pepper
salt

Preheat oven to 450°F. Remove giblets and excess fat from chicken cavity. Rinse and remove excess moisture with paper towels. Rub cavity with salt and pepper and place 2 tablespoons butter within, or rub with oil. Dry outside of chicken thoroughly with paper towels. This will aid browning. Truss chicken as shown on page 26. Rub outside with 2 tablespoons butter or oil. Sprinkle salt and pepper on outside of bird. Place chicken on its **side** on rack in roasting pan. Rack allows even heat circulation

around bird during roasting. Place pan with chicken in middle of heated oven. **Roast chicken at 450°F. for entire roasting time** (see timetable, page 30). Melt remaining butter in skillet over medium heat. After 1/3 of total roasting time (15 minutes in this case), baste chicken with butter. Turn bird onto its other side without piercing skin. After 2/3 of time has elapsed, turn bird onto its back and baste with juices at bottom of roasting pan. Near the end of the cooking time, insert instant-registering meat thermometer into thickest part of thigh. When 170°F. is registered, chicken is perfectly cooked. Remove from oven and let rest 10 minutes before carving. This allows juices to settle into flesh. The rich pan drippings are all the sauce that is needed. Remove trussing strings before carving. Makes 4 servings.

FAST-ROASTING TIMETABLE

CHICKEN WEIGHT (Ready to Cook)	OVEN TEMP.	COOKING TIME (Unstuffed)	COOKING TIME (Stuffed)
3/4 to 1 pound	450°F.	25 to 30 minutes	30 to 35 minutes
1-1/2 to 2 pounds	450°F.	35 to 40 minutes	40 to 50 minutes
2-1/2 to 3 pounds	450°F.	45 to 50 minutes	55 to 60 minutes
3-1/2 to 4 pounds	450°F.	50 to 60 minutes	65 to 75 minutes
4-1/2 to 5 pounds	450°F.	55 to 65 minutes	70 to 80 minutes
5-1/2 to 6 pounds	450°F.	65 to 75 minutes	75 to 85 minutes

ROASTING A STUFFED CHICKEN

Here's the basic recipe for those who prefer chicken stuffed.

Stuffing, your choice (see pages 36 through 39)
1 chicken, 4-1/2 to 5 lbs.

4 tbs. butter or margarine
salt and pepper

Prepare stuffing according to desired recipe. Allow to cool to room temperature. Loosely fill chicken cavity. Do not overstuff. Stuffing will expand as it absorbs juices during cooking. (Extra stuffing can be baked in separate pan.) Truss the chicken according to directions on page 26. Rub outside of chicken with 2 tablespoons of butter. Sprinkle with salt and pepper. Preheat oven to 450°F. Lay chicken on its side on rack in roasting pan. Place in oven. Melt remaining butter. After 1/3 of total roasting time has elapsed, baste chicken with butter and turn onto other side, being careful not to pierce skin. Roast for another 1/3 of total time. Baste with pan drippings and turn bird on its back. Roast for final 1/3 of cooking time. Near the end of the cooking time test for doneness in the thickest part of the thigh with an instant-registering thermometer (should register 170°F.). Remove from oven and let rest 10 minutes before carving.

Modern Roast Chicken

HOW TO CARVE A ROAST CHICKEN

Let chicken rest at room temperature for 15 minutes before carving. This allows the juices to settle into the flesh. Remove trussing strings.

(1) Place chicken breast side up. Insert fork into leg, gently pull leg while cutting skin all around. Pierce the joint that connects the leg and thigh to the carcass, and separate from the body. Do likewise with the other leg.

(2) Holding chicken with the fork through the breast, cut through the shoulder joint where the wing and the body are connected. Cut off as little breast meat as possible when removing the wing.

(3) To carve breast, hold chicken firmly in place by pressing fork into breastbone on the half that you are going to carve. Slice down diagonally through the meat. Lift off each slice as you cut it.

FLAVORED BUTTERS FOR ROAST CHICKEN

For additional interest, flavored butter can be used in place of plain butter to heighten the flavor of basic roast chicken. To make flavored butter, always start with cold butter. It will become fluffy when beaten. Warm butter, on the other hand, will become oily and slick. Spices and herbs other than those suggested can also be used.

FLAVORED BUTTER MASTER RECIPE

1/2 cup cold butter
flavoring ingredients (any of the suggestions on page 35)

Beat butter until fluffy. Beat in additional ingredients. If unsalted butter is used, add 1/4 teaspoon salt. Omit if butter is salted. Refrigerate 10 to 15 minutes before use. Will flavor 1 to 2 chickens.

Prepare according to the directions for the Flavored Butter Master Recipe on the preceding page.

PARSLEY BUTTER

1/2 cup cold butter
1/2 cup fresh chopped parsley
1/4 tsp. freshly ground pepper

GARLIC BUTTER

1/2 cup cold butter
3 to 4 cloves of garlic, crushed
1/4 tsp. freshly ground pepper

LEMON-CURRY BUTTER

1/2 cup cold butter
1 to 2 tsp. curry powder
2 tsp. grated lemon rind
1/4 tsp. freshly ground pepper

GINGER BUTTER

1/2 cup cold butter
1 tbs. ground ginger
1/4 tsp. ground cinnamon
1 garlic clove, crushed
1 tsp. soy sauce
1/4 tsp. freshly ground pepper

Modern Roast Chicken

STUFFINGS FOR ROAST CHICKEN

Here are my favorites. Each one is quite different from the other. All are easy to prepare and delicious.

SIMPLE BREAD STUFFING

1/4 cup butter
1/4 cup chopped onion
1/2 tsp. sage

1/8 tsp. salt
1/4 tsp. pepper

4 cups dry bread crumbs
1 cup chicken broth

Melt butter in saucepan over medium heat. Saute onions in butter until tender. Add sage, salt and pepper. Combine with bread crumbs. Add broth, tossing well. Produces enough stuffing for a 4-1/2 to 5 pound bird. Can be baked in covered casserole at 325°F. for 45 minutes.

Apple-Nut Stuffing Variation: saute 1/4 cup chopped celery with onion. Add 1 peeled, cored and chopped apple, 1/2 cup slivered almonds and 1/4 cup raisins to stuffing before filling chicken.

BRANDIED-PECAN STUFFING

A rich taste and nutty texture recommend this spirited stuffing.

1 cup apple juice
1/4 cup apricot or peach-flavored brandy
1/4 cup butter or margarine
1 pkg. (8 ozs.) corn bread stuffing mix
3/4 cup pecans

Combine juice, brandy and butter in saucepan. Place over medium heat. Stir until butter melts. Add stuffing mix and pecans, tossing lightly to blend. Produces enough stuffing for a 4-1/2 to 5 pound chicken. Can be baked in covered casserole at 325°F. for 45 minutes.

Modern Roast Chicken

CRANBERRY-ORANGE STUFFING

A festive, autumn stuffing.

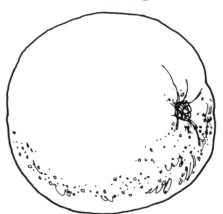

2/3 cup chopped fresh cranberries
2 tbs. sugar
2 tsp. grated orange peel
1/2 tsp. salt
1/4 tsp. ground cinnamon
3 cups dried raisin bread cubes
2 tbs. melted butter or margarine
1/4 cup orange juice

Combine cranberries, sugar, orange peel, salt and cinnamon in bowl. Add bread cubes and drizzle with melted butter and orange juice. Stir lightly to mix. Produces enough stuffing for a 4-1/2 to 5 pound chicken. Can be baked in covered casserole at 325°F. for 45 minutes.

SAVORY RICE AND MUSHROOM STUFFING

6 tbs. butter or margarine
2 cups diced celery
1 cup diced onions
1 cup chopped fresh mushrooms
2 cups cold cooked brown or white rice
1/4 tsp. salt
1/4 tsp. pepper
1/4 tsp. rubbed sage
1/4 tsp. thyme leaves

Melt butter in skillet over medium heat. Saute celery, onions and mushrooms until tender, about 5 minutes. Stir frequently. Add remaining ingredients. Mix well. Produces enough stuffing for a 4-1/2 to 5 pound chicken. Can be baked in covered casserole at 325° F. for 25 minutes.

Apricot Rice Stuffing: Add 1 cup snipped dried apricots. Omit mushrooms and sage.

Modern Roast Chicken

PLUM DELIGHTFUL ROAST CHICKEN

1 chicken, 3-1/2 to 4 lbs.
1-1/4 cups herb stuffing mix
1 apple, peeled and finely chopped
1/3 cup finely chopped celery
9 tbs. hot water, divided
3 tbs. margarine, melted
2 tbs. chopped walnuts

1 tbs. finely chopped onion
1/2 cup dry white wine
1/2 cup plum jam
1/4 cup lemon juice
1-1/2 tsp. ground ginger
1/4 tsp. salt
2 tbs. flour

Rinse chicken and dry well with paper towels. In large bowl, combine stuffing mix, apple, celery, 5 tablespoons water, margarine, walnuts and onion. Loosely fill cavity of chicken. Truss chicken as directed on page 26. Place chicken on rack in large shallow baking pan. Combine wine, jam, lemon juice, ginger and salt. Brush over chicken. Roast in low 325° F. oven (because sauce burns easily) about 1-3/4 hours or until thermometer registers 170° F. when inserted into thickest part of thigh. Remove chicken to serving platter. Skim fat from pan juices. Combine flour and remaining 4 tablespoons water and stir into pan juices. Cook, stirring, over medium heat until thickened. Serve with chicken. Makes 4 servings.

Modern Roast Chicken

SUCCULENT BROILED OR BARBECUED CHICKEN

BROILING AND BARBECUING CHICKEN

Broiling and barbecuing are both methods of cooking in which radiant heat is used to cook food quickly. When chicken is broiled or barbecued, the moistest and tastiest results are achieved if intense heat causes the outside of the chicken to become brown and crisp while allowing natural juices to remain sealed in. Contrary to common belief, it is this browning, together with the intensity of heat, that gives barbecued chicken its special flavor and character and not the taste of the charcoal.

To insure that the sealing and browning process occurs properly during barbecuing or broiling, the following procedures should be applied: The chicken joints should be broken so that the pieces will lay flat and all the meat will be at about the same distance from the heat source. If no marinade or barbecuing sauce is being used the chicken should be dried with paper towels and then basted with a thin layer of oil before cooking. The oil will assist in creating a screen which seals in the natural juices, but allows the heat to enter and cook the meat. Basting during broiling or barbecuing continues to protect this seal. Next, the chicken pieces should be placed close enough to the heat source to permit the intense heat to seal and brown the meat, but just far enough away to avoid burning. Frequent monitoring and adjusting of the distance may be necessary, until a thorough familiarity with a given heat source is acquired. Ingredients in the barbecue or basting sauce may require further adjustment of the cooking distance. For example, honey or sugar based sauces can char more easily than others. When using a charcoal grill, chicken can usually be placed 2 to 3 inches from the coals, while in an oven broiler, the distance is more variable (3 to 6 inches) depending on the broiler design. Tongs rather than a fork should always be used for turning. The tongs will not pierce the skin and cause the seal to break.

If a **charcoal grill** is used, an even, intense heat source will be created by a full bed of charcoal briquettes which have burned until they become glowing coals covered with a layer of gray ash. If an **oven broiler** is used, preheat the broiler (but not the broiling pan) for 5 to 10 minutes.

Cooking time for chicken pieces on a charcoal grill is about 25 to 30 minutes per side. In an oven broiler, the chicken will cook in 15 to 20 minutes per side. Testing for doneness should be performed with an instant-registering meat thermometer. White meat is done when the thermometer registers 140°F. and dark meat is done at 165°F.

BASIC OVEN-BROILED CHICKEN

Intense heat from the broiler causes the outside of chicken to become brown and crisp while allowing natural juices to remain sealed in.

1 chicken, 2-1/2 to 3 lbs., cut into halves or quarters
salt and pepper
1/2 cup vegetable oil, melted butter or a basting sauce

Preheat broiler 5 to 10 minutes with door slightly ajar. Wash chicken and pat dry with paper towels. Season with salt and pepper. Brush generously with oil, butter or basting sauce. Arrange chicken skin side up on rack over shallow roasting pan. Place 3 to 4 inches below preheated broiling unit. Broil 10 to 15 minutes on each side. Baste often to seal skin and keep chicken juicy. Turn with tongs. Adjust chicken to a distance of 5 to 6 inches from broiler unit so that it will cook and brown without burning. Broil 10 to 15 minutes longer, turning once or twice more, basting each time. Test for doneness with an instant-registering thermometer. White meat is done when internal temperature reaches 140° F. Dark meat is done at 165° F.

BASIC GRILLED OR BARBECUED CHICKEN

Oil, butter or a basting sauce assist in creating a screen which seals in natural juices, but allows the intense heat to enter and cook the meat.

1 chicken, 2-1/2 to 3 lbs., cut into halves or quarters
salt and pepper
1/2 cup vegetable oil, melted butter or a basting sauce

Preheat electric grill or have a bed of glowing coals covered with a layer of gray ash ready. (It may take the coals 30 minutes to 1 hour to be ready for cooking.) Wash chicken and pat dry with paper towels. Season with salt and pepper. Brush generously with oil, butter or a basting sauce. Place chicken skin side down on the grill 2 to 3 inches above heat source. Grill 10 to 15 minutes on each side. Baste often to seal skin and keep chicken juicy. Turn with tongs. Raise grill to about 4 inches from heat. Grill 10 to 15 minutes longer, turning once or twice more, basting each time. Test for doneness with an instant-registering thermometer. White meat is done when internal temperature reaches 140° F. Dark meat is done at 165° F.

CARAWAY CHICKEN HALVES

1/2 cup vegetable oil
1/4 cup light corn syrup
1/4 cup chopped onion
1 tbs. lemon juice
1 tsp. dried oregano
1 tsp. caraway seed
1/4 tsp. salt
2 chickens, 2 to 2-1/2 lbs. each, split in half, lengthwise

Combine oil, syrup, onion, lemon juice, oregano, caraway seed and salt in bowl. Mix well. Marinate chicken in mixture. Remove from marinade. Broil under preheated oven broiler, 3 to 6 inches from heat source, a total of 15 to 20 minutes on each side **or** barbecue over **slow** coals 25 minutes. Turn, barbecue 20 minutes more, brushing occasionally with sauce. Continue barbecuing, 10 minutes more, or until meat is tender. Turn occasionally and brush with marinade. Makes 4 servings.

CHICKEN TERIYAKI

Teriyaki-style barbecuing originated in Japan.

1/2 cup soy sauce
1 clove garlic, minced
2 tbs. sugar
2 tbs. fresh ginger, minced
1/2 cup orange juice (fresh, if possible)
3 tbs. vegetable oil
1/4 cup sherry
1 chicken, 2-1/2 to 3 lbs. cut into serving pieces

Mix together soy sauce, garlic, sugar, ginger, orange juice, oil and sherry in bowl. Toss chicken in this mixture to coat well and marinate 1 to 2 hours at room temperature. Turn at least twice while marinating. Reserve marinade. Broil or barbecue for 15 minutes on each side. Remove chicken from heat and replace in marinade for an additional 30 minutes to absorb more flavor. Finish by barbecuing or broiling each piece 10 to 15 minutes more on each side. Makes 4 servings.

Broiled & Barbecued

TEXAS BARBECUED CHICKEN

A good all-purpose barbecue sauce. Try it on ribs too.

1/4 cup butter or margarine, melted
1/4 cup molasses
1 garlic clove, crushed
1/2 tsp. paprika
2 tbs. tarragon vinegar
3/4 cup catsup
1 tbs. Worcestershire sauce

1 tsp. mustard
1/4 tsp. salt
1/4 tsp. pepper
2 chickens, 2-1/2 to 3 lbs. each
    cut into halves
salt and pepper
chili powder

Combine butter, molasses, garlic, paprika, vinegar, catsup, Worcestershire, mustard, salt and pepper in saucepan. Simmer 20 minutes over low heat. Stir occasionally. Rub chicken with salt, pepper and chili powder. Brush generously with sauce. Place skin sides up, 3 inches from hot coals or skin sides down in preheated oven broiler. Broil 25 to 30 minutes on each side over coals or 15 to 20 minutes in broiler. Baste with sauce often. Makes 4 to 6 servings.

BRANDY CHICKEN FOR ONE

1 chicken leg-thigh combination
2 tbs. butter or margarine, melted
1 tsp. brandy
1/8 tsp. garlic powder
dash cayenne pepper
1/8 tsp. seasoning salt

In a shallow baking dish, mix together butter, brandy, garlic powder and cayenne. Add chicken, turning to coat evenly. Sprinkle with half of seasoning salt. Place chicken skin side up on broiler pan. Broil about 6 inches from broiling unit for 10 minutes. Turn, brush with any remaining butter mixture and sprinkle with remaining seasoning salt. Broil about 15 minutes more or until tender. Makes 1 serving.

Broiled & Barbecued

UNCOMMON CHICKEN CASSEROLES

BARBECUED CHICKEN CASSEROLE

Be sure to serve French bread to go with the extra sauce.

1 chicken, 2-1/2 to 3 lbs.
 cut into serving pieces
seasoned flour
vegetable oil
1/2 cup finely chopped onion
1/2 cup finely chopped celery
1/2 cup finely chopped green pepper
2 tbs. butter or margarine

2 tbs. vinegar
2 tbs. brown sugar
1/4 cup lemon juice
1 cup catsup
3 tbs. Worcestershire sauce
1-1/2 tsp. prepared mustard
1/4 tsp. salt
1 cup water

Coat chicken with seasoned flour. Brown in small amount of oil. Remove chicken pieces to shallow baking dish or casserole. Saute onion, celery and green pepper in butter. Add remaining ingredients. Simmer 20 minutes. Pour sauce over chicken. Bake, uncovered, at 350°F. for 1 hour or until chicken is tender. Makes 4 servings.

Chicken Casseroles

CHICKEN HACIENDA

1/2 cup all-purpose flour
1/2 tsp. salt
1/2 tsp. pepper
1/2 tsp. paprika
1 chicken, 2-1/2 to 3 lbs.,
   cut into serving pieces
2 tbs. vegetable oil
4 strips bacon, cooked

2 carrots, sliced
1 can (4 ozs.) chopped green chilies
1 tbs. chopped fresh parsley
1 bay leaf
1/2 tsp. thyme
1 lemon, thinly sliced
2 cups tomato juice

Combine flour, salt, pepper and paprika in bowl. Roll chicken pieces in seasoned flour. Pour oil into large skillet. Place over medium-high heat. Add chicken pieces and brown well on all sides. Drain and remove chicken to large casserole dish. Lay bacon strips over chicken. Add carrots, chilies, parsley, bay leaf and thyme to casserole. Top with lemon slices and pour tomato juice over all. Cover and bake at 350°F. for 1 hour. Skim and discard fat before serving. Makes 4 servings.

CHILI CHICKEN CASSEROLE

1 chicken, 2-1/2 to 3 lbs., cut into serving pieces
1 can (16 ozs.) tomatoes
1 can (8 ozs.) tomato sauce
1 tbs. vinegar
2 tsp. chili powder
1/2 tsp. salt, divided

1 clove garlic, minced
1 can (15 ozs.) New Orleans style
red kidney beans, undrained
1 small onion, sliced
1 green pepper, diced

Place chicken in 3-quart mixing bowl. Sprinkle with 1/4 teaspoon salt. In another bowl, mix together tomatoes, tomato sauce, vinegar, chili powder, 1/4 teaspoon salt and minced garlic. Stir in kidney beans, onions and green pepper. Pour mixture over chicken. Cover and marinate overnight in refrigerator. When ready to cook, place chicken, skin side up, in single layer in large shallow baking pan. Bake, uncovered, in 350° F. oven for about 1 hour, or until chicken is tender. Serve on rice or noodles. Makes 4 servings.

Chicken Casseroles

CHICKEN-VEGETABLE CASSEROLE

The frozen orange juice concentrate adds a special tang to this tasty casserole.

1/2 cup all-purpose flour
1/2 tsp. salt
1/4 tsp. pepper
1 tbs. paprika
1 chicken, 2-1/2 to 3 lbs.,
    cut into serving pieces
2 tbs. vegetable oil

1 can (8 ozs.) whole onions, drained
1/2 cup chopped carrots
1 can (8 ozs.) sliced mushrooms
1 tbs. sugar
1/3 cup frozen orange juice concentrate,
    thawed

Mix flour, salt, pepper and paprika together in bag. Shake chicken pieces, 2 at a time, in mixture. Reserve 2 tablespoons of leftover flour mixture. Heat oil over medium-high heat in large skillet. Add chicken and brown well on all sides. Remove chicken to baking dish together with onions, carrots and mushrooms. Add reserved flour and sugar to skillet, stirring until smooth paste is formed. Add juice concentrate and 3/4 cup water. Cook until bubbly, stirring constantly. Pour over chicken. Cover and bake at 350°F. for 1-1/2 hours. Makes 4 servings.

CREAMY BAKED CHICKEN

1/4 cup all-purpose flour
1/2 tsp paprika
1/2 tsp. salt
1/4 tsp. pepper
1/4 tsp. poultry seasoning
1 chicken, 2-1/2 to 3 lbs.,
    cut into serving pieces
1/4 cup butter or margarine
1 can (10-1/2 ozs.) cream of chicken soup
1/2 cup milk, whole or lowfat
1 tbs. chopped fresh parsley

Mix together flour, paprika, salt, pepper, and poultry seasoning in a bowl. Coat chicken pieces with mixture. Melt butter and pour into shallow baking dish. Arrange chicken in single layer in dish. Bake 30 to 40 minutes at 350°F., turning once. Combine soup and milk. Pour over chicken and sprinkle with parsley. Bake 30 to 40 minutes more. Makes 4 servings.

POPOVER CHICKEN-TARRAGON CASSEROLE

Children love the puffy, flaky "pastry" that tops this baked chicken stew.

1 tbs. vegetable oil
1 chicken, 2-1/2 to 3 lbs.,
    cut into serving pieces
1/4 tsp. salt
1/4 tsp. pepper
3 eggs

1-1/2 cups milk, whole or lowfat
2 tbs. melted butter or margarine
1-1/2 cups all-purpose flour
1 tsp. dried tarragon
1/4 tsp. salt

Pour oil into large skillet. Place over medium-high heat. Add chicken and brown well on all sides. Sprinkle with salt and pepper. Place chicken in greased, shallow 2-quart baking dish. In mixing bowl, beat eggs. Add milk and melted butter. Mix well. Stir flour, tarragon and salt into egg mixture. Beat until smooth. Pour over chicken. Bake at 350°F. for 60 to 70 minutes. Makes 4 servings.

CHICKEN AND SAUERKRAUT CASSEROLE

4 strips bacon
1/3 cup all-purpose flour
1/4 tsp. salt
1/8 tsp. pepper
1 chicken, 2-1/2 to 3 lbs.,
    cut into serving pieces
1 cup chopped onion

1 clove garlic, crushed
1/2 tsp. thyme
2 tbs. all-purpose flour
1-1/2 cups chicken stock
1 can (16 ozs.) sauerkraut, drained
1 tbs. sugar

Fry bacon in skillet until crisp. Remove and drain on paper towels. Crumble bacon when cool. Reserve bacon drippings. Mix flour, salt and pepper together in bowl. Roll chicken in mixture. Place chicken in bacon drippings over medium-high heat. Brown pieces well on all sides. Remove chicken and set aside. Add onion, garlic and thyme to skillet. Saute until onion is tender. Blend in flour and cook 1 minute, stirring constantly. Gradually add chicken broth. Cook, stirring, until mixture thickens. Stir in bacon, sauerkraut and sugar. Bring to boil. Pour into 3-quart casserole dish. Cover with chicken pieces. Bake at 350°F. for 50 to 60 minutes. Skim and discard fat before serving. Makes 4 servings. **Please note:** Chicken may be browned in vegetable oil instead of bacon drippings if desired.

CROCK POT CHICKEN AND SAUSAGE

Put this dish into the crock pot before leaving in the morning, and dinner is ready and delicious when you return at night.

2 carrots, cut into 1/2" slices
1 onion, chopped
1/2 cup water
1 (6 ozs.) can tomato paste
1/3 cup red table wine
1 tsp. garlic powder

1/2 tsp. crushed thyme
1/4 tsp. ground cloves
3 bay leaves
2 (16 ozs. each) cans navy beans, drained
4 chicken breast halves, skinless, frozen
1/2 lb. polish sausage, fully cooked, sliced into 1/4" pieces

In a small saucepan, bring water, carrots and onions to a boil. Reduce heat and simmer for 5 minutes. Pour mixture into a 4-quart crock pot cooker. Stir in tomato paste, seasonings, wine and beans. Place frozen chicken breasts on top of mixture and add sausage slices. Cover and cook on low heat for 9-10 hours (or high heat for 6 hours). When ready to serve, remove bay leaves and skim fat from dish. Serve with a green salad and crusty French bread. Serves 4.

SAVORY CHICKEN SOUPS

HOMEMADE CHICKEN BROTH OR BOUILLON

Chicken broth or bouillon is stronger than chicken stock. Stock is made using only bones and vegetables. Broth can be made by reducing stock or by starting with the entire chicken. If only broth is desired, use chicken meat for salads or other cooked chicken dishes.

1 stewing chicken, 4 to 5 lbs.
6 cups cold water
1 carrot, sliced
1 onion, sliced
2 celery stalks, with leaves
1/2 bay leaf
6 whole peppercorns
1/2 tsp. salt

Put all ingredients in Dutch oven. Bring to boil, cover and lower heat. Simmer 2 hours. Remove chicken. Cool broth. Skim and discard fat. Strain broth. Makes about 1 quart.

CHICKEN CONSOMME

Consomme comes from the French word meaning "to boil down." It is a strong soup made by reducing broth and then clarifying to make it sparkling clear. An appropriate curtain raiser for any formal meal.

1 recipe Homemade Chicken Broth, page 60

To make consomme, reduce broth by boiling uncovered to one half its original volume. When reduced, clarify consomme in the following manner: For each quart of consomme place 2 egg whites **and** their crushed shells in large bowl. Beat until frothy and about double their original volume. Pour beaten egg whites and shells into consomme and bring back to rolling boil, stirring. Immediately remove from heat and allow to rest 5 to 10 minutes. This will allow egg whites and shells to rise to top. The impurities in the soup will be clinging to them. Next, line a wire strainer with a damp layer of muslin or cheesecloth. Place strainer over a large bowl. Gently ladle consomme into strainer. Soup will slowly drip through cloth and be clear. Re-heat and serve immediately. Note: if desired, consomme can be chilled until jellied, and served on a bed of lettuce, garnished with sprig of parsley or watercress.

CHICKEN AND CUCUMBER SOUP

A fresh, crunchy soup that's quick to prepare. Taste a small piece of cucumber before you add them to the soup. If they are bitter, throw them away. Use only mild and sweet cucumbers in this soup.

2 whole cucumbers
1 cup chopped cooked chicken
4 cups chicken broth
3 tbs. sherry

Wash and peel cucumbers. Cut each cucumber lengthwise and remove the seeds with a spoon. Discard seeds. Cut cucumbers into thin slices. Bring chicken broth to a boil in a large saucepan. Add chopped chicken and cucumbers. Simmer for 15 minutes. Add sherry and correct seasonings. Serve hot or cold. Makes 4 to 6 servings.

CHICKEN CORN CHOWDER

This chowder originated in the Midwest, where corn fields abound. Here's a delicious modern version.

4 strips bacon
1 cup chopped onion
2 cups cubed potatoes
2 cups chicken broth
2 cups diced cooked chicken

1 can (8 ozs.) whole kernel corn, drained
1 can (8 ozs.) cream-style corn
1 cup light cream or milk
1/4 tsp. pepper
chopped fresh parsley

Fry bacon in skillet until crisp. Drain on paper towels. When cool, crumble. Drain and discard all but 2 tablespoons drippings. Saute onions in skillet over medium heat in drippings until tender, about 8 to 10 minutes. In Dutch oven combine onions, potatoes and chicken broth. Bring to boil. Reduce heat and simmer until potatoes are tender, about 15 minutes. Add chicken, whole corn, cream-style corn, light cream and pepper. Heat thoroughly. Garnish each serving with crumbled bacon bits and parsley. Makes 4 to 6 servings. **Please note:** Onions may be sauteed in vegetable oil instead of bacon drippings, if desired.

CHICKEN GUMBO

Creole gumbos are dishes which use okra for flavoring and thickening. Okra is a bean or seed pod, which is the color of string beans, but about 3 to 4 inches in length. The pods have ridges which make slices of okra appear slightly octagonal in shape. Believed to have originated in West Africa, they were brought to the United States during the slave trade.

1 tbs. butter or margarine
1 onion, finely chopped
1/2 cup celery, finely chopped
4 cups chicken broth
1/2 green pepper, finely chopped

1 cup cooked or canned okra
1/2 cup chopped, cooked chicken
1/2 tsp. salt
1/2 tsp. pepper
1 can (16 ozs.) tomatoes

Melt butter in skillet over medium heat. Saute onion and celery in butter for 7 to 8 minutes, stirring constantly. Add chicken broth, green pepper, okra, chicken, salt, pepper, and tomatoes. Bring to boil, then reduce heat and simmer for 45 minutes. Makes 4 to 6 servings.

CHILLED SENEGALESE CHICKEN SOUP

3 tbs. butter or margarine
2 onions, chopped
2 stalks celery, chopped
2 apples, peeled, cored and chopped
1 to 1-1/4 tbs. curry powder
1/4 cup all-purpose flour

4 cups chicken broth
dash chili powder
salt
2 cups light cream or milk
3/4 cup diced, cooked chicken, chilled

Melt butter in large saucepan over medium heat. Saute onion, celery and apples 6 to 8 minutes, stirring occasionally. Add curry powder, cook, stirring for a few minutes. Do not allow curry to brown. Add flour; cook 1 minute, stirring constantly. Stir in chicken broth gradually. Cook, stirring constantly, until slightly thickened. Add chili powder and salt. Cool slightly. Pour into blender jar and puree. Chill. Before serving, stir in light cream and chilled chicken meat. Makes 6 servings.

COCK-A-LEEKIE SOUP

A rich soup of Scottish origin. The prunes add a delicate and slightly sweet flavor.

2 lbs. boneless beef shank
3 dozen leeks
1 stewing chicken, 4 to 5 lbs.
3 quarts cold water
1/2 tsp. salt
1 tsp. pepper
1 cup pitted prunes, cut into small pieces

Cut beef into 5 or 6 pieces. Wash leeks very well, making sure to remove sand. Slice them thinly, including 3 inches of the darker green leaves. Put chicken, beef, leeks, water, salt and pepper into a Dutch oven. Simmer 3 hours. Check occasionally. Remove beef and chicken. Add prunes; simmer one hour longer. When meats are cool, remove bones and skin from chicken and gristle from beef. Dice meats. Return to soup. Skim fat. Simmer 15 minutes longer. Makes 8 to 10 servings.

CHICKEN GIBLET SOUP

1 lb. giblets (hearts and gizzards only)
4 cups chicken broth
3 tbs. butter
1 onion, chopped
1 celery stalk, chopped
1/2 green pepper, chopped
1 garlic clove, minced
2 tbs. all-purpose flour
1 tsp. prepared mustard
salt and pepper

Rinse giblets. Pour broth into large saucepan. Add giblets and simmer 1 hour. Melt butter in saucepan over medium heat. Saute onion, celery, pepper and garlic until tender, about 6 to 8 minutes. Reduce heat. Add flour. Cook 2 minutes, stirring constantly. Remove giblets from saucepan. Slice giblets and return to broth. Stir in sauteed vegetables and mustard. Add salt and pepper. Cook one minute longer, serve hot. Makes 4 servings.

Savory Soups

MEMORABLE CHICKEN STEWS

CHICKEN SIMMERED IN BEER

1/4 cup butter or margarine
1 chicken, 2-1/2 to 3 lbs., cut into serving pieces
salt and pepper
6 green onions, finely chopped
1 large carrot, grated
1 bay leaf
1/4 tsp. dried thyme
1 bottle (12 ozs.) beer
1 cup stewed tomatoes, drained
1 tbs. flour

Melt butter in skillet over medium-high heat. Add chicken, sprinkle with salt and pepper, and saute on all sides. Add green onions, carrot, bay leaf and thyme. Sprinkle with 1/2 teaspoon salt. Pour in beer. Cover and reduce heat. Simmer until chicken is tender, about 1-1/2 hours. Remove to warm platter. Skim and discard fat. Add tomatoes. Mix flour with 4 tablespoons water until lumps disappear and add to sauce. Cook until thickened. Serve chicken covered with sauce. Makes 4 servings.

Chicken Stews

CHICKEN CACCIATORE

This chicken, simmered in a rich, red sauce, is best served over hot spaghetti. The trick to cooking perfect spaghetti noodles or any pasta is to pour about a tablespoon of oil into the boiling, salted water with the pasta. Test frequently during cooking. All pasta should be cooked just until it offers only the slightest resistence to your teeth, when you bite it. This is called "al dente."

Complete this meal with a tossed green salad, French bread and dry red wine.

1 chicken, 2-1/2 to 3 lbs.,
    cut into serving pieces
1 cup all-purpose flour
3 tbs. olive oil
3 tbs. butter or margarine
1 medium-sized onion, chopped
1/2 lb. small mushrooms, sliced
2 tsp. chopped fresh parsley

1 clove garlic, mashed
1 cup dry white wine
1 can (10-3/4 ozs.) spaghetti
    sauce with mushrooms
2 bay leaves
1/2 tsp. salt
1/2 tsp. pepper
4 ozs. dry spaghetti

Dredge chicken pieces in flour, coat well on all sides. Heat olive oil in large skillet over medium-high heat. Saute chicken until well browned on all sides. Remove chicken from skillet and set aside. Add butter to skillet. Saute onion and mushrooms until lightly browned, about 5 minutes. Add parsley, garlic and wine. Stir to scrape browned bits from bottom of skillet. Return chicken to skillet. Cover and simmer 10 minutes. Add spaghetti sauce, bay leaves, salt and pepper. Cover and simmer 35 minutes, or until chicken is tender. Remove bay leaves. Skim and discard fat. Meanwhile, cook the spaghetti in boiling, salted water until it is just tender, or "al dente." Drain spaghetti well. To serve, arrange noodles on a serving platter. Place chicken on top of noodles and spoon sauce over the chicken pieces. Makes 4 servings.

Chicken Stews

CHICKEN CALABRIAN

One of Italy's classic chicken dishes. On an attractive platter, the figs, orange slices and parsley create tremendous visual appeal.

2 chickens, 2-1/2 to 3 lbs. each,
    quartered
1/4 cup olive oil
1/2 tsp. salt
1 tsp. dried oregano
2 tsp. minced fresh parsley

2 cloves garlic, minced
1 cup dry white wine
3 tbs. lemon juice
1 can (17 ozs.) Kadota figs, drained
1 orange cut into 1/4-inch slices
1/2 cup sherry

Brush chicken with olive oil. Combine salt, oregano, parsley and garlic in a bowl. Mix well. Roll chicken in mixture. Place in shallow baking dish, skin side up. Bake, uncovered at 400°F. for 50 to 55 minutes, turning once during cooking. Combine wine and lemon juice. Use to baste chicken often during cooking. Meanwhile, prick figs with fork. Marinate figs and orange slices in sherry while chicken cooks. Five to ten minutes before chicken is done, skim and discard fat. Add figs and orange slices. Makes 4 servings.

CHICKEN PAPRIKA

3 chicken legs
3 chicken breasts
1/4 cup all-purpose flour
1/4 tsp. salt
2 tbs. oil
1/4 cup diced onions

3/4 cup hot water
2 tsp. lemon juice
3 tbs. all-purpose flour
1-1/2 cups sour cream
2 cups cooked noodles
2 tsp. paprika

Skin, bone and remove fat from chicken. Cut pieces in half. Combine 1/4 cup flour and salt in a bowl. Roll chicken in mixture. Heat oil in large skillet on medium-high heat. Add chicken and brown well on all sides. Add onions, hot water and lemon juice. Cover, and simmer 40 minutes until chicken is tender. Skim and discard fat. Blend 3 tablespoons flour with 1/2 cup of sour cream. Blend into chicken mixture. Stir in remaining sour cream and noodles. Simmer 5 minutes. Add paprika and mix well. Serve hot. Makes 6 servings.

Chicken Stews

CHICKEN STEW WITH DUMPLINGS

1 stewing chicken, 4-1/2 to 5 lbs.,
   cut into serving pieces
2 onions, sliced
5 carrots, sliced
3 to 4 celery ribs
2 whole cloves garlic, peeled

1 bay leaf
1 tsp. thyme **OR** sage
1/2 tsp. salt
1/2 tsp. pepper
chicken stock (about 4 cups)
Dumplings (next page)

Place all ingredients in a very large pot or Dutch oven. Add enough stock to completely cover chicken. Bring to boil, partially cover and simmer for 2 to 2-1/2 hours, or until chicken is tender. Skim and discard fat from cooking liquid every 30 minutes. Start preparing dumpling batter about 30 minutes before stew is done. Using a large tablespoon, drop dough directly onto chicken in boiling stew. Cover and return to boil. Lower heat. Simmer 12 to 15 minutes without lifting cover. Remove dumplings and chicken to platter. Spoon broth over dumplings before serving. Makes 6 to 8 servings.

DUMPLINGS

Try these dumplings in beef stew too.

1 cup all-purpose flour
2 tsp. baking powder
1/4 tsp. salt
2 tbs. snipped fresh parsley
1 egg
1/3 cup milk
2 tbs. butter or margarine

Prepare dumplings about 30 minutes before chicken stew is done. Stir together flour, baking powder and salt. Add parsley. Mix egg, milk, and melted butter together. Add to flour mixture, stirring until just blended. Cook with chicken as directed in preceding recipe.

CHICKEN STEW, CORSICAN-STYLE

A simple and piquant dish. Do not add any salt until the dish is finished cooking. The bacon and olives impart a saltiness of their own.

4 tbs. olive oil
1 whole roasting chicken,
   about 3 lbs.
5 slices bacon, diced
1/4 lb. whole button mushrooms

1 cup pitted green olives, drained
1 lb. tomatoes, chopped
1/4 cup brandy
1 lb. new potatoes, peeled
sugar, salt and pepper

Pour 2 tablespoons of oil in Dutch oven or large skillet. Place over medium-high heat. Brown whole chicken on all sides. After chicken has sauteed for 5 minutes, add bacon and mushrooms. Cook 5 to 10 more minutes. Add olives, tomatoes and brandy. Cover and simmer for 1 hour, or until chicken is tender. Meanwhile, in frying pan, brown new potatoes lightly in remaining 2 tablespoons of olive oil. Add potatoes to Dutch oven. Cook for another 1/2 hour. Transfer to a serving dish. Skim and discard fat from sauce. Add sugar, salt and pepper to taste. Pour sauce over chicken and serve. Makes 4 servings.

76

Chicken Baked in
Tomato-Almond Puree (page 134) ►

CHICKPEA-LEMON CHICKEN STEW

The turmeric lends this whole, stewed chicken a lovely golden-yellow color.

1 whole chicken, 3-1/2 to 4 lbs.,
    cut into serving pieces
3 tbs. vegetable oil
1 onion, finely chopped
4 cloves garlic, minced
2 tsp. turmeric

1/2 tsp. **EACH** salt and pepper
1 to 2 quarts chicken stock
1 can (15 ozs.) chickpeas or garbanzo beans
juice of two lemons

In Dutch oven heat oil to medium-high. Add onion and garlic. Saute until translucent, about 4 minutes. Add 1 teaspoon turmeric, salt and pepper. Cook one more minute. Rub chicken with remaining turmeric. Add chicken pieces to pot and sear on all sides until golden-yellow. Add just enough stock to cover chicken. Add chickpeas and lemon juice. Bring to boil. Reduce heat and simmer until done, about 1-1/2 hours. Makes 4 servings.

FRIED CHICKEN STEW

A hearty chicken stew which originated in Mainland China. Particularly satisfying on a cold day.

8 dry Chinese mushrooms
4 cups chicken stock
1/2 cup soy sauce
1/2 tsp. minced ginger
2 tbs. sugar
1 chicken, 1-1/2 to 3 lbs.,
    boned and cut into bite-sized pieces

1 cup all-purpose flour
vegetable oil for frying
2 bell peppers, cut into eighths
1 head Chinese or regular cabbage,
    cut into 1-inch pieces
2 scallions

Place mushrooms in small bowl. Cover with water. Let soak at room temperature for 1 hour. Drain. Slice finely. In large saucepan bring stock, soy sauce, ginger and sugar to boil. Dredge chicken in flour. Heat about 2 inches of oil in deep saucepan to medium-high (375°F.). Deep fry chicken pieces for 3 to 5 minutes. Remove and place chicken in simmering stock. Add mushrooms, bell peppers and Chinese cabbage. Serve in bowls and garnish with chopped scallions. Makes 4 servings.

NEW BRUNSWICK CHICKEN STEW

The addition of the bananas to this typically New England style dish gives it a Latin American flavor. Once cooked in the stew, their flavor more closely resembles potatoes than bananas.

1 chicken, 2-1/2 to 3 lbs.,
   cut into serving pieces
1 tsp. salt
10 peppercorns
1 tbs. minced onion
1 bay leaf

1 can (28 ozs.) tomatoes
1 pkg. (10 ozs.) frozen corn
1 pkg. (10 ozs.) frozen lima beans
1 tsp. dried basil, crumbled
2 green-ripe bananas

Place chicken, salt, peppercorns and onion in a large kettle or Dutch oven. Cover all with 2 quarts of water. Bring to a boil for 15 to 20 minutes. Skim and discard fat. Strain broth. Add tomatoes, corn, lima beans and basil to kettle, along with 3 cups of strained broth. Return to boil. Remove skin and bones from chicken, dice meat. Peel and cut bananas into 1/2-inch chunks. Add chicken and bananas to stew. Cover and simmer 30 to 35 minutes. Makes 6 servings.

Chicken Stews

CHICKEN BREASTS SUPREME

BASIC CHICKEN BREAST CUTLETS

Here are some tips for producing perfect chicken breast cutlets. Pound them thin, being careful not to tear them. Saute the cutlets quickly, so that they stay tender and succulent. It is extremely important not to dry out the breasts by overcooking.

2 chicken breasts, skinned,
    boned and halved
1/4 cup all-purpose flour
salt and pepper
1 egg

1/2 cup bread crumbs
3 tbs. butter
2 tbs. cognac or brandy (optional)
parsley and lemon wedges for garnish

Place each breast half between 2 pieces of waxed paper. Flatten to thickness of 1/4 inch. Mix flour, salt and pepper together in a bowl. In another bowl, beat egg. Dip each breast in flour mixture, then egg, then crumbs. Chill at least one hour before sauteing. Melt butter in large skillet over medium-high heat. Add breasts and saute 3 to 4 minutes, turning occasionally. If desired, warm cognac in separate pan. Pour over breasts. Carefully ignite. Gently shake pan until flames subside. Garnish with parsley and lemon wedges, if desired. Makes 4 servings.

Chicken Breasts Supreme

BAKED CHICKEN BREASTS REUBEN

2 chicken breasts, boned and halved
2 tbs. butter or margarine
1/4 tsp. salt
1/4 tsp. pepper

3/4 cup bottled Thousand Island dressing
1 can (16 ozs.) sauerkraut, drained
4 slices natural Swiss cheese
1 tbs. minced parsley

Pat chicken breasts dry with paper towels. Melt butter in frypan over medium-high heat. Saute breasts until nicely browned. Remove breasts and place in buttered baking dish. Sprinkle with salt and pepper. Spread about 1 tablespoon of dressing over each breast. Squeeze excess juice from sauerkraut. Cover breasts with sauerkraut. Spoon a little more dressing on top of sauerkraut. Cover dish with foil and bake at 350° F. about 30 minutes or until breasts are tender. Remove from oven and uncover. Top with cheese and spoon remaining dressing over cheese. Return to oven for about 5 minutes or until cheese is melted. Sprinkle with parsley and serve. Makes 4 servings.

CHICKEN BREASTS A LA NORMANDE

Serve over cooked rice, noodles or mashed potatoes.

2 chicken breasts, skinned,
   boned and halved
flour
1/4 cup oil
3/4 cup brandy (preferably apple brandy)

1/2 cup whipping cream
2 tsp. butter or margarine
2 small green apples
2 to 4 tbs. sugar

Peel, core and slice apples thinly. Set aside. Roll breasts in flour. Heat oil in skillet to medium-high. Add breasts and saute 1 to 2 minutes per side, or until golden. Remove breasts and discard oil. Add 1/2 cup brandy to skillet and return breasts. Place over high heat, **ignite carefully**, then immediately cover to put out flame. Again, remove breasts. Add cream to skillet and reduce liquid, by boiling, to half of its original volume. Add butter and shake pan until butter melts. Stir sugar and remaining brandy into skillet. Add apple slices. Bring to boil and cook one minute. Place breasts on warm serving plate, surround with apples and top with sauce. Makes 4 servings.

Chicken Breasts Supreme

CHICKEN BREASTS PICATTA

The Madeira, lemon juice and capers form a piquant counterpoint to the breasts.

2 chicken breasts, skinned,
   boned and halved
1/4 cup all-purpose flour
1/4 tsp. salt
1/4 tsp. paprika
3 tbs. olive oil

2 tbs. butter
2 tbs. Madeira wine
2 tbs. lemon juice
1/2 lemon, thinly sliced
2 tbs. capers
2 tbs. chopped fresh parsley

Place each breast half between 2 pieces of waxed paper and flatten to thickness of 1/4 inch with mallet. Mix together with flour, salt and paprika in plastic bag. Shake each breast in bag. Heat oil and butter in large skillet over medium-high heat. Saute breasts 2 minutes on each side, or until golden. Remove to warm platter. Drain and discard all but two tablespoons butter mixture. Add Madeira to skillet. Cook over medium heat, stirring to dissolve bits which have adhered to skillet bottom. Add lemon juice. Heat briefly. Return breasts and lemon slices to re-heat. Add capers and parsley; serve. Makes 4 servings.

CHICKEN BREASTS IN RUM CRUMBS

A warm, buttery delight! The crusty covering of "rum crumbs" surrounds the chicken breasts. These envelope a chestnut and chutney filling.

2 chicken breasts, skinned, boned and halved
1/4 cup **PLUS** 1 tbs. rum
1/2 cup breadcrumbs
1/4 cup butter
2 tbs. chutney, with liquid
2 tbs. pureed marrons (chestnut spread)

Place each breast half between 2 pieces of waxed paper and flatten to thickness of 1/4 inch with mallet. Pour 1/4 cup rum into small bowl. Dip each chicken breast half into rum, then into crumbs. Melt butter in skillet over medium-high heat. Saute each chicken one minute per side, until golden. Meanwhile, mix chutney and marron with 1 tablespoon rum. Warm in small saucepan. Spread mixture onto half of chicken pieces. Top with other sauteed chicken pieces. Serve hot. Makes 4 servings.

Chicken Breasts Supreme

CHICKEN BREASTS SAVOYARDE

A truly sumptuous recipe. My wife's favorite.

Sauce (see next page)
2 tbs. vegetable oil
1 tbs. butter or margarine
1 medium onion, sliced
1 tsp. dried tarragon
1/2 tsp. thyme

4 chicken breasts, skinned boned and halved
1/2 cup dry white wine
1/4 tsp. salt
1/4 tsp. pepper
1 can (8 ozs.) artichoke bottoms
1/4 cup chopped parsley

Prepare sauce and set aside. In large skillet, heat oil and butter over medium-low heat. Add onion, tarragon and thyme. Cook until onions are tender, about 8 to 10 minutes, stirring frequently. Add breasts, about half at a time. Do not crowd them or they won't brown properly. Saute 6 to 8 minutes, turning once. Add wine, salt and pepper. Cover and simmer 5 minutes more. Heat artichoke bottoms gently in their own liquid, drain. Arrange chicken breasts in shallow lightly greased baking dish. Place artichokes around chicken. Pour sauce over chicken. Place under broiler to heat through and brown, about 5 minutes. Sprinkle with parsley. Makes 8 servings.

Chicken Breasts Supreme

SAUCE

1 tbs. butter or margarine
1 tbs. all-purpose flour
3/4 cup dry white wine
1/2 cup chicken broth
1/2 cup sour cream
1/2 cup grated Parmesan cheese
1/2 tbs. prepared mustard
1/4 tsp. pepper

In saucepan, melt butter over medium heat. Stir in flour. Cook, while stirring constantly, until mixture bubbles for 30 seconds. Gradually stir in white wine, chicken broth and sour cream. Simmer 5 minutes, or just until boiling. Add cheese, mustard and pepper. Simmer 5 minutes more, stirring. Remove from heat. Use as directed in recipe above.

Chicken Breasts Supreme

CHICKEN BREASTS STUFFED WITH GOAT CHEESE AND BASIL

This unique recipe will get rave reviews from dinner guests.

3 whole chicken breasts, boned, split
3 ozs. mild goat cheese
6 fresh basil leaves
salt and pepper
1/2 cup crab-apple jelly, for glaze

Carefully loosen skin from each chicken breast and insert 1 tablespoon cheese and one basil leaf under it. Pull skin back over meat and tuck underneath it. Place breasts in a buttered baking dish, barely touching each other. Brush each with jelly and roast in a preheated 375°F. oven for 30 minutes, or until breasts are golden brown. Cool slightly and slice into medallions. Serves 5-6.

CHICKEN WITH WINES AND SPIRITS

BAKED ORANGE-RUM CHICKEN

A great dish to serve on a warm summer's evening. The combination of rum and orange flavoring are reminiscent of Caribbean cuisine.

1/4 cup rum
2 tbs. butter
2 tbs. firmly packed brown sugar
2 tbs. frozen orange juice concentrate
1/4 tsp. salt
1/8 tsp. pepper
1/4 tsp. ground ginger
1 chicken, 2-1/2 to 3 lbs., cut into serving pieces

In small saucepan combine rum, butter, brown sugar, orange juice concentrate, salt, pepper and ginger. Place over medium heat, until sugar dissolves. Brush pieces of chicken with mixture. Arrange chicken, skin side up, in a large shallow baking dish. Bake, uncovered at 375°F. for 50 to 60 minutes, basting once with rum mixture during baking process and once again just before serving. Makes 4 serving.

CHICKEN AMARETTO

Lovers of the almond-flavored liqueur "Amaretto" will especially like this simple recipe. They won't have to wait until after dinner to savor its goodness.

6 chicken breast halves,
   boned and skinned
1/2 tsp. salt
1/2 tsp. pepper
1/4 tsp. **EACH** garlic powder and curry powder
1/4 cup **EACH** flour and butter or margarine

1/2 lb. fresh mushrooms, sliced
1/4 cup Amaretto liqueur
grated rind and juice of 1 lemon
1 tbs. cornstarch
1-1/2 cups chicken broth

Cut chicken into 1-inch wide strips. Mix salt, pepper, garlic powder, curry powder and flour together in plastic bag. Shake chicken pieces in bag with mixture. Melt butter in a large skillet over medium-high heat. Add chicken pieces and saute quickly. Reduce heat to medium-low. Add mushrooms, Amaretto, lemon rind, and juice. Simmer 5 minutes. Mix cornstarch and 2 tablespoons water to form paste. Blend paste with chicken broth. Stir mixture into skillet with chicken. Cook over low heat, stirring constantly until mixture bubbles and thickens. Makes 6 to 8 servings.

CHICKEN BREASTS MADEIRA

A good sherry can be used, but Madeira wine makes a difference worth trying. Use it if possible!

2 chicken breasts, skinned,
  boned and halved
salt
paprika

3 tbs. butter
3/4 cup heavy cream or half and half
1/4 cup Madeira wine
12 mushrooms, sliced

Season chicken breasts with salt. Dust lightly with paprika. Melt 2 tablespoons butter in frypan over medium heat. Brown breasts lightly on all sides. Remove from pan. Add remaining butter and melt. Blend in 1 cup cream and Madeira. Return breasts to pan. Cook, uncovered, very slowly until tender, about 20 minutes. Stir in remaining cream and mushroom slices. Simmer very slowly 10 to 15 minutes longer. Makes 4 servings.

CHICKEN-HAM MARSALA

Marsala wine compliments this creamy combination of chicken and ham.

1/4 lb. cooked ham, finely chopped
6 large chicken thighs, bones removed
2 tbs. butter, melted
1/2 cup sliced mushrooms
1 can (10 ozs.) cream of mushroom soup

1 cup (1/2 pint) sour cream or
   sour half and half
1/2 cup Marsala wine
2 tsp. paprika
1 tbs. cornstarch mixed with 2 tbs. water

Divide chopped ham into 6 portions. Fill inside of chicken thighs with ham. Fold over to close, and tie, skin side out, with string (or secure with skewers). Pour butter into a 9-inch square baking dish. Roll chicken in butter and place in dish. Combine mushrooms, soup, sour cream and Marsala in saucepan. Place over medium-high heat, stirring constantly. As soon as mixture begins to bubble, remove it from heat. Pour mixture over chicken. Sprinkle with paprika. Bake uncovered at 450°F. for 15 minutes. Cover and reduce heat to 350°F. Bake 30 minutes more. Remove chicken to serving platter. Pour sauce into saucepan. Simmer until warm. Add cornstarch paste. Stir until thickened. Pour over chicken and serve. Makes 4 to 6 servings.

CHICKEN THIGHS WITH SHERRY STUFFING

8 chicken thighs, skinned
3 slices bacon
4 tbs. butter or margarine
1/2 cup finely chopped celery
1/2 cup finely chopped onion

4 tbs. sherry wine
1/8 tsp. poultry seasoning
1/4 tsp. pepper
2 cups soft bread crumbs
1/8 tsp. salt

Remove bones from thighs by cutting thighs almost in half along bone. Cut around bone with sharp knife and remove it. In small frypan over medium heat, cook bacon until crisp. Drain, crumble and set aside. Melt 2 tablespoons butter in frypan. Add celery and onion. Saute about 5 minutes. Remove from heat. Add 2 tablespoons sherry, poultry seasoning, pepper, bread crumbs and bacon. Stir until mixed. Fill each boned thigh with 2 tablespoons of filling mixture. Roll up and fasten with wooden picks. Arrange stuffed thighs in shallow casserole. Combine remaining butter and sherry. Brush thighs well with mixture and sprinkle with salt. Bake at 450° F. 5 minutes. Reduce heat to 350° F. and bake about 45 minutes or until chicken is tender. Baste once or twice with butter mixture.

CHICKEN A LA BRANDYWINE

8 chicken thighs, skinned and boned
1/4 tsp. salt
1/4 tsp. paprika
5 tbs. butter, divided
4 ounces ham, diced
4 slices pineapple, halved

1/4 cup chopped scallions
1 tbs. brandy, warmed
1/2 cup white wine
1 tbs. plus 1 tsp. flour
1/2 cup heavy cream
1/4 cup slivered almonds

Rinse thighs and dry with paper towels. Sprinkle with salt and paprika. In large frypan, melt 2 tablespoons butter over low heat. Add thighs. Top with pineapple slices, ham and scallions. Cover and cook about 45 minutes or until chicken is tender. (Do not let brown.) Pour warmed brandy over chicken. Touch with lighted match to flambe. Transfer contents of frypan, as undisturbed as possible, to a warm platter and keep warm. Add wine to frypan and cook over high heat about 2 minutes. Mix flour and cream until smooth. Stir into wine. Simmer until thickened. Add 1 tablespoon of butter to sauce and stir until melted. In small frypan, saute almonds in remaining butter until light brown. To serve, spoon part of sauce over chicken. Serve remaining sauce in separate dish. Makes 4 servings.

With Wines & Spirits

SPIRITED CHICKEN IN CLAY

This recipe was especially designed for the popular clay roasting dishes. Chicken is flavorful, moist and delicious prepared this way.

1/2 tsp. salt
1 roasting chicken, 4 to 5 lbs.
1/4 cup butter or margarine
1 tbs. **PLUS** 1 tsp. grated orange rind
3 tbs. lime juice

1 tsp. Worcestershire sauce
2 tbs. orange liqueur
1/3 cup **PLUS** 1 tbs. orange marmalade
2 tbs. brandy

Salt cavity of chicken. Melt butter in large skillet over medium-high heat. Add chicken and saute on all sides. Remove chicken from heat. Combine orange rind, lime juice, Worcestershire sauce, orange liqueur, marmalade and brandy. Pour over chicken and let stand one hour. Soak clay crockery dish in water for 10 minutes. Line dish with foil because sugar in recipe will encrust bottom. Place chicken in dish. Cover tightly and roast chicken at 400°F. for one hour. Spoon sauce over chicken and roast 30 minutes more. Makes 4 to 6 servings.

CHICKEN FLAVORED WITH HERBS AND SPICES

CHICKEN WITH VINEGAR SAUCE

A very good, fresh tasting sauce that is mildly piquant.

1 chicken, 3 to 4 lbs.,
   cut into serving pieces
1 cup all-purpose flour
1/2 tsp. EACH salt and pepper
1/2 cup butter or margarine
1 onion, chopped

4 cloves garlic, chopped
1 tbs. tomato paste
1/2 cup tarragon-flavored vinegar
1/2 cup white wine
veal or beef stock
1 tbs. Dijon mustard

Roll chicken pieces in flour which has been mixed with salt and pepper. In deep skillet melt half of butter over medium-high heat. Saute chicken in butter until lightly browned. Add onion, garlic, tomato paste, vinegar and wine. Add enough stock to barely cover chicken. Bring to boil. Reduce heat, cover and simmer 30 minutes. Next, transfer chicken to warm serving dish. Skim and discard fat. Correct seasonings and return liquid to boil. Remove from heat. Stir in remaining butter and mustard. Pour sauce over chicken and serve. Makes 4 servings.

GINGER AND ANISE CHICKEN

3/4 cup soy sauce
1 tbs. honey
1/2 cup firmly packed brown sugar
1-1/2 cups water
2 tbs. minced fresh ginger
3 cloves garlic, minced

1 star anise (if available)
1/4 cup chopped green onions
2 tbs. sherry
1 chicken 2-1/2 to 3 lbs., whole
2 tbs. cornstarch mixed with 4 tbs. water

Combine soy sauce, honey, brown sugar, water, ginger, garlic, star anise, green onions and sherry in large cooking pot. Bring to boil. Simmer, stirring for 2 minutes. Add chicken, including liver and gizzard. Cover and simmer 40 minutes, or until chicken is tender. Remove chicken from pot and let stand at room temperature for 30 minutes to cool. Remove flesh from bones. Discard bones. Cut into bite-sized pieces with cleaver or sharp knife. Arrange on platter. Add cornstarch paste to sauce. Bring to boil. Simmer until mixture thickens. Pour over chicken. Makes 4 servings.

With Herbs & Spices

GARLIC CHICKEN

Although an entire head of garlic is used in this recipe, it does not overpower the dish. Simmering the garlic lessens its pungent flavor.

1 chicken, 3 lbs., cut into serving pieces
salt and pepper
3 tbs. butter
1 whole head of garlic (12 to 15 cloves)

1/2 tsp. dried rosemary
1/3 cup dry white wine
1/2 cup chicken stock
chopped fresh parsley for garnish

Sprinkle chicken with salt and pepper. Melt butter in large ovenproof skillet over medium-high heat. Saute chicken pieces until lightly browned. Cover skillet and place in a 375°F. oven for 8 minutes. Meanwhile, peel all garlic cloves, leaving them whole. Place whole cloves in small saucepan. Add enough water to just cover garlic. Simmer for 25 minutes. Drain, being careful not to mash cloves. Add garlic, rosemary and wine to chicken. Return to oven and bake an additional 25 minutes. Remove skillet from oven. Arrange chicken and garlic on heated platter. Keep warm in 200°F. oven. Skim and discard all except 4 tablespoons of fat from skillet. Add chicken stock to skillet. Boil uncovered until reduced to one-half its origianl volume. Stir to dissolve the brown bits clinging to bottom of pan. Add garlic cloves, simmer gently for 2 minutes. Pour over chicken. Garnish with chopped parsley. Serve immediately. Makes 4 servings.

MUSTARD SURPRISE CHICKEN

The surprise in this recipe is that the two cups of mustard create an easy-to-make dish which has a mild and delicate taste.

1 frying chicken, 2-1/2 to 3 lbs., cut into serving pieces
2 cups inexpensive prepared mustard (not Dijon)
salt and pepper

Dredge chicken in mustard, coating each piece thoroughly. Sprinkle with salt and pepper. Bake in shallow, uncovered, greased baking dish for one hour at 350°F. Mustard will have formed a puff pastry-like shell around each piece of chicken. Makes 4 servings.

SOUR CREAM BAKED CHICKEN

A simple dish whose rich sour cream and mustard sauce qualifies it as a company meal. Prepare it with a gourmet mustard for a special treat.

1/2 cup sour cream or sour half and half
1/4 cup prepared mustard
1/2 tsp. salt
1/4 tsp. rosemary leaves, crushed
1/8 tsp. black pepper
2 chickens, 3 lbs. each, cut into serving pieces
2-1/2 cups fresh bread crumbs
1/2 cup melted butter or margarine

Combine sour cream, mustard, salt, rosemary and pepper. Mix well. Spread mixture over chicken pieces, coating well. Roll chicken in bread crumbs. Arrange in shallow baking dish. Drizzle with half of butter. Bake at 375°F. for 30 minutes. Remove from oven and drizzle with remaining butter. Bake 30 minutes more, or until chicken is golden brown and done. Makes 6 to 8 servings.

INTERNATIONAL CLASSICS

CHICKEN KIEV

12 tbs. butter (3/4 cup)
3 eggs
2 tbs. water

6 whole chicken breasts, skinned,
   boned and halved (see page 12)
about 2 cups finely crumbled dry bread crumbs
vegetable oil for frying

Slice butter into 12 pieces, each about 2 inches x 1/4 inch. Chill until hard. Beat eggs and water together in bowl. Place each breast between two sheets of waxed paper. Pound with a mallet until 1/4-inch thick. Trim and discard any ragged edges. Roll each pounded breast around 1 slice of butter. Fold the right and left sides over and secure with toothpicks. Do this carefully. It's important that the butter not leak during the cooking process. Roll bundle in bread crumbs. Dip in beaten egg mixture. Roll in crumbs again. Refrigerate for at least 1 hour. Heat about 2 inches of oil in a deep skillet to medium-high, or 350°F. Carefully slip 3 or 4 bundles into the hot oil at a time. Don't try and fry them all at once. It's important not to crowd them, because the temperature of the oil will drop causing the chicken to cook too slowly and become greasy. Fry the bundles from 6 to 8 minutes, or until dark brown. Drain on paper towels. Keep warm in 200°F. oven while others fry. Makes 6 servings.

ARUBA CHICKEN

This flavorful dish is perfect for guests — a real taste treat!

2 tbs. olive oil
1 medium brown onion, sliced
1 (3 lbs.) fryer, cut into serving pieces
1 (1 lb.) smoked pork butt,
   cut into 1" cubes
1 (8 ozs.) can tomato paste
1/4 cup coconut, shredded
1/2 tsp. salt

1/2 tsp. crushed red pepper (or to taste)
4 whole cloves
1 bay leaf
1/2 tsp. thyme
2 lbs. sweet potatoes, pared, cut into
   1/2" slices
2 bananas, sliced 3/4" thick
1/4 cup green onions, sliced

Heat oil in a heavy Dutch oven and saute onion about 5 minutes until golden, stirring frequently. Remove from pan. Add chicken, half at a time, and brown on all sides (adding more oil if needed). Return onion to pan and add pork. Stir in water, tomato sauce, coconut and salt. Tie pepper, cloves, bay leaf and thyme into a small cheesecloth square (poultice) and add to stew. Bring to a boil, lower heat and simmer for 15 minutes, stirring occasionally. Add sweet potatoes and simmer covered for 35 to 40 minutes longer, or until sweet potatoes are tender. Taste for seasonings and correct if necessary. Add bananas and cook for additional 5 minutes. Discard cheesecloth poultice. Arrange on a serving platter and garnish with green onions and more coconut, if desired. Serves 6.

International Classics

PAELLA VALENCIANA

Worth travelling to Spain to eat. But you can cook it at home and feel as if you are in Valencia. A great party dish!

1/3 cup olive oil
1 chicken, 2-1/2 to 3 lbs.,
    cut into serving pieces
1/2 lb. pork, diced
1/2 tsp. salt
1/2 tsp. pepper
1 onion, chopped
1/4 tsp. saffron
2 cloves garlic, minced
1 green pepper,
    seeded and chopped

3 medium tomatoes, chopped
1-1/2 cups uncooked rice
3 cups chicken stock
1/2 lb. fresh or
    1 pkg. frozen green peas
3 pimientos, sliced
1/2 lb. firm-flesh fish fillets, cubed
3/4 lb. raw shrimp,
    shelled and deveined
10 to 12 clams, well scrubbed

In large Dutch oven heat olive oil to medium-high. Add chicken and pork. Saute until well browned. Remove with slotted spoon. Add salt, pepper, onion, saffron, garlic and green peppers. Saute until browned. Add tomatoes, rice and chicken stock. Cover and simmer 5 minutes. Return chicken and pork to Dutch oven. Cover and cook 30 minutes. Add peas, pimientos, fish and shrimp. Cover and cook 10 minutes. Meanwhile, prepare clams in separate saucepan. Place clams in saucepan with 1/2-cup water. Cover and cook over medium heat 6 to 8 minutes. Reduce heat and discard any clams that have not opened. Arrange clams in the stew. Makes 8 servings.

DEEP FRIED CHICKEN

Everyone's favorite. Although there are scores of variations, this is one of the best.

1 cup all-purpose flour
1/2 tsp. salt
1 tsp. black pepper

1 chicken, 2-1/2 to 3 lbs.
    cut into serving pieces
lard or vegetable oil for frying (about 3 to 4 cups)

Mix flour, salt and pepper in large bowl. An hour before cooking, do not wipe chicken dry, but directly coat each piece of chicken by rolling in flour. Place pieces on wire rack and allow to stand at room temperature for 1 hour. Place a cookie sheet covered with absorbent paper towels in oven. Heat oil to 350°F. (use a frying thermometer) in deep saucepan equipped with frying basket. There should be enough fat to completely cover chicken pieces immersed in it. Carefully drop dark meat pieces into hot fat. Fry 10 to 12 minutes, turning occasionally with tongs. When done, place pieces in oven on cookie sheet to keep warm while frying remaining chicken. Fry white meat pieces for 8 to 9 minutes each, turning occasionally. Serve on warm platter. Makes 4 servings.

CHICKEN COOKED IN BURGUNDY WINE (COQ AU VIN)

1/2 cup butter or margarine
3 slices bacon, finely chopped
1 medium onion, finely sliced
1 chicken, 2-1/2 to 3 lbs., cut
    into serving pieces
1 tbs. flour
2 tbs. brandy
2 cups dry red wine

1 bay leaf
1/4 tsp. dried thyme
1 tbs. chopped fresh parsley
1/2 tsp. salt
1/2 tsp. pepper
1/8 tsp. ground nutmeg
1 cup chopped mushrooms,
    sauteed in butter

Melt 1/4 cup butter in a Dutch oven over medium heat. Saute bacon and onion until transparent, about 5 minutes. Remove bacon and onion with slotted spoon and reserve. Add chicken and brown on all sides in remaining fat. Sprinkle with flour. Add brandy, wine, bay leaf, thyme, parsley, salt, pepper and nutmeg. Cover and bake at 350°F. for 40 minutes. Skim and discard fat. Stir in reserved onion, bacon and mushrooms. Cover and return to oven. Bake 5 to 10 minutes more. Stir remaining butter into sauce. Serve with noodles or mashed potatoes. Makes 4 servings.

◀ Chicken Cacciatore (page 70)

International Classics

CHICKEN MOLE

Justifiably, one of Mexico's most famous dishes. The bitter chocolate, toasted seeds and spices blend together to make a very rich, thick sauce for the chicken.

4 tbs. vegetable oil
2 chickens, 3 lbs. each,
    cut into serving pieces
1/4 cup sesame seeds
1 cup sliced almonds
1/3 cup pumpkin seeds
2 heat and serve (crispy) taco shells
1 cup onions, chopped
2 cloves garlic

1 can (16 ozs.) tomatoes
2 cups chicken broth
1 tsp. cinnamon
1 oz. grated bitter (baking) chocolate
2 tsp. finely minced chili pepper
salt and pepper
1 tbs. sugar
2 tbs. lime juice

Pour 2 tablespoons oil in large skillet. Heat to medium-high. Add chicken pieces and brown on all sides. Remove chicken to large shallow baking dish. Cook sesame seeds, almonds and pumpkin seeds in skillet over medium heat until brown, stirring constantly. Place nuts and seeds in blender jar and puree. Add taco shells to jar. Puree again. Add remaining 2 tablespoons of oil to skillet. Saute onions and garlic until well browned. Add to blender jar. Finally, add tomatoes, broth, cinnamon, chocolate, chili, salt, pepper, sugar and lime juice to blender jar. Puree again. Pour sauce over chicken. Cover and bake 1 hour at 375°F. Skim and discard fat. Serve with sauce spooned over chicken. Makes 8 servings.

International Classics

ORIENTAL DELICACIES

BASIC STIR-FRIED CHICKEN

1 chicken breast, boned and skinned
2 slices fresh ginger root, peeled
1 scallion
1 tbs. cornstarch
1 tbs. **EACH** sherry and water
1 lb. vegetables (celery, broccoli, mushrooms, water
    chestnuts, peas, onions, bamboo shoots, bean
    sprouts; in any combination desired)

3 tbs. vegetable oil
1 tbs. soy sauce
1/2 tsp. sugar
1 tsp. salt
1/2 cup chicken stock

Slice chicken into thin pieces. Mince ginger root and scallion. Combine with cornstarch, sherry and water. Add to chicken. Toss to coat and let stand 15 minutes. Meanwhile, slice desired vegetables. Pour 1-1/2 tablespoons oil in skillet or wok. Heat to high. Stir-fry chicken 2 to 3 minutes and remove from skillet. Heat remaining 1-1/2 tablespoons oil. Add vegetables and stir fry 1 to 2 minutes. Sprinkle with soy sauce, sugar and salt. Stir in stock. Simmer until vegetables are crisp-tender. Return chicken to reheat. Serve at once. Makes 4 servings.

Oriental Delicacies

CHICKEN SAUTEED WITH HOISIN SAUCE AND GREEN PEPPERS (SZECHUAN)

This exciting dish will make you think you are eating in your favorite Szechuan Chinese restaurant.

1/4 tsp. salt
2 tsp. cornstarch
2 tsp. sherry
3/4 lb. raw boned chicken, diced
1/4 cup vegetable oil

1 tbs. Hoisin sauce (or substitute 2 tbs. catsup)
2 dried mushrooms, soaked and diced
1 green pepper, diced
1/2 tsp. red chili pepper, minced
1/2 cup bamboo shoots, diced

Mix salt, cornstarch and sherry. Add chicken and stir to coat well. Heat oil in skillet or wok until quite hot. Saute chicken over high heat 2 minutes. Remove chicken. Add Hoisin sauce to skillet. Cook one minute more. Add mushrooms, green pepper, chili pepper and bamboo shoots. Saute one minute. Return chicken to skillet to reheat. Serve immediately. Makes 4 servings.

CHICKEN VELVET AND PEAS

A smooth variation of basic stir-fried chicken. Serve it over rice. A fruit salad will round out the meal nicely.

2 chicken breasts, boned and skinned
2 tbs. chopped fresh ginger
3 scallions, chopped
1 tsp. sherry
2 tsp. soy sauce
6 egg whites

2 tbs. cornstarch
1/3 cup vegetable oil
6 ozs. peas or snow peas
1/4 cup chicken stock
2 ozs. cooked ham, minced

Mince chicken breasts finely. Mix ginger, scallions, sherry, soy sauce, egg whites and cornstarch until mixture is smooth. Heat oil in skillet or wok until quite hot. Add peas and stir fry 2 minutes (one minute for snow peas). Add chicken stock. Continue to cook, stirring 1-1/2 minutes. Add chicken-egg mixture. Stir fry over high heat about 2 minutes, breaking up any lumps. Serve mixture on heated platter, garnished with minced ham. Makes 4 servings.

Oriental Delicacies

SIMMERED JAPANESE CHICKEN BREASTS

This is a teriyaki-type of dish that doesn't require a broiler or grill. Make a big batch; the leftovers are great served cold over hot, steaming rice. This is a good dish for a crowd, too.

2 chicken breasts, skinned, boned and halved
1/3 cup vegetable oil
1/3 cup soy sauce
1/4 cup sugar
1 tsp. minced fresh ginger

Bring two cups water to boiling over medium-high heat in large saucepan. Plunge breasts into boiling water for 30 seconds. Drain. Heat oil in skillet until quite hot and brown the breasts for 2 to 3 minutes. (If you are doubling or tripling the recipe, brown only 2 chicken breasts at a time). Remove breasts and pour off oil. Add soy sauce, sugar and ginger to skillet. Cook covered 5 to 6 minutes. Remove cover and simmer until sauce is syrupy. Slice breasts and serve hot or cold. Makes 4 servings.

ROYAL PEACOCK SILVER WRAPPED CHICKEN

1 chicken breast, skinned and boned
1/4 tsp. salt
1 tsp. sugar
3 tbs. Hoisin sauce
   (may substitute 4 tbs. catsup)
1/4 tsp. Chinese 5 spice powder
   (substitute mixture of cinnamon and
   ground ginger if 5 spice not available)

1/2 tsp. sesame oil
2 tbs. all-purpose flour
3 tbs. vegetable oil
6 leaves cilantro, minced
1 clove garlic, minced
sixteen 4-inch squares of
   aluminum foil
vegetable oil for frying

Cut breast into 16 pieces. Combine salt, sugar, Hoisin sauce, 5 spice powder, sesame oil, flour, oil, cilantro and garlic. Add chicken, mix well and marinate 2 hours. Wrap each piece of chicken in 4-inch square of foil. Be sure to roll edges of foil twice so juices do not escape. Heat about 2 inches of oil in deep saucepan to medium-high (375°F.). Deep fry each packet 7 minutes. Remove with slotted spoon. Unwrap and serve as appetizer. Makes 4 to 6 appetizer servings.

Oriental Delicacies

CHINESE LEMON CHICKEN

Takes a bit of time to prepare, but the results are well worth the effort. These delicious morsels of chicken taste similar to scallops when prepared this way. Great served as an appetizer. Simply place the cubes in an attractive bowl next to a dish of toothpicks.

1 lb. chicken, boned,
    skinned and diced
1/8 tsp. salt
2 tbs. egg custard mix (powder)
1/4 tsp. pepper
1/2 tsp. soy sauce
1 tbs. white wine

2 tsp. water
Lemon Sauce (see next page)
1/3 cup cornstarch
1 egg beaten
1/4 cup peanut oil
lemon slices for garnish

Marinate chicken for 30 minutes in mixture of salt, egg custard mix, pepper, soy sauce, wine and water. Meanwhile, prepare Lemon Sauce. Just before cooking chicken, add cornstarch and egg to chicken mixture. Heat oil until it is quite hot in wok or skillet. Add chicken mixture and stir fry 2 to 3 minutes until golden brown. Arrange on serving platter. Bring Lemon Sauce to boil; pour over chicken. Garnish with lemon slices. Makes 4 servings.

LEMON SAUCE

1/2 tsp. cornstarch
2 tsp. egg custard mix (powder)
3 tsp. sugar
1/4 cup lemon juice
1/2 tsp. white vinegar

3 tbs. water
1/4 tsp. salt
1/4 tsp. sesame oil
3 lemon slices, halved

   Combine cornstarch, custard mix and sugar in small suacepan. Add lemon juice, vinegar, water, salt and sesame oil. Add lemon slices. Bring to boil. Pour over cooked chicken.

PAPER WRAPPED CHICKEN

Wrapped chicken recipes are usually served as appetizers. The following two recipes are good examples of Chinese hors d'oeuvres cuisine.

4 dried Chinese mushrooms
1/2 lb. raw chicken, boned and diced
2 tbs. soy sauce
1 tbs. dry sherry
1 tbs. sugar

sixteen 6-inch squares of waxed paper
2 tsp. fresh peeled and minced ginger
3 scallions, cut into 1-1/2-inch lengths
vegetable oil for deep frying

Place mushrooms in small bowl. Cover with water. Let soak at room temperature for 1 hour. Drain. Slice finely and set aside. Marinate chicken in mixture of soy sauce, sherry and sugar for 1 hour. On each square of waxed paper put a heaping table-spoon of a combination of the following ingredients: chicken, ginger, mushrooms and scallions. Fold paper like an envelope, tucking in flap. Put parcels, flap side down, on plate. Heat 2-inches of oil in a deep saucepan to medium-high (375°F.). Fry parcels, 1/2 at a time, for 3 minutes each. Drain. Return all parcels together to hot fat and fry an additional 1-1/2 minutes. Serve immediately. Serves 4 as an appetizer.

CHICKEN COOKED WITH FRUIT

Chicken With Fruit

CHICKEN IN WINE AND FRUIT SAUCE

2 chicken breasts, skinned
  boned and halved
1/2 cup flour
1/4 tsp. salt
1/4 tsp. pepper
1/4 cup oil
1/2 cup chopped onion
2 cloves garlic, minced

1/2 cup slivered almonds
1 cup orange juice, unsweetened
1/2 cup crushed pineapple, drained
1/4 cup raisins
2 tbs. sugar
1/2 tsp. cinnamon
1/8 tsp. ground cloves
1 cup white wine

Roll breasts in a mixture of the flour, salt and pepper. Heat oil in frypan over medium-high heat. Add breasts and saute 1 to 2 minutes per side or until golden brown. Arrange in a buttered casserole. Saute onion, garlic and almonds in the same oil. Add remaining ingredients EXCEPT wine. Pour sauce over chicken. Cover casserole and bake at 320° F. for 20 minutes. Uncover casserole, turn chicken and pour wine overall. Increase temperature to 350° F. and bake 15 minutes longer. Serve with steamed rice. Makes 4 servings.

APRICOT GLAZED CHICKEN

The ease with which this dish is prepared belies its elegant appearance and rich flavor.

1 cup bottled Russian salad dressing
1/4 cup vegetable oil
1 pkg. (1-3/4 ozs.) dry onion soup mix
1 cup apricot preserves
3 tbs. lemon juice
1/2 tsp. salt
2 chickens, 3 lbs. each, cut into serving pieces

Mix together salad dressing, oil, soup mix, preserves, lemon juice and salt. Arrange chicken pieces in shallow baking dish. Pour preserve mixture over chicken. Bake for 1 hour at 350°F., or until chicken is tender. Baste twice while baking. Makes 6 to 8 servings.

Chicken With Fruit

CHICKEN WITH PAPAYA

This dish reminds one of the Hawaiian Islands, but eliminates the plane fare.

2 garlic cloves, split and speared with toothpicks
2 tbs. margarine
1 (2-3 lbs.) fryer, cut into serving pieces
1/2 tsp. salt
2 ripe papayas, halved, seeds removed, sliced
1 cup chicken broth, heated to boiling

Cook garlic in heated margarine until golden; remove. Add chicken pieces and ginger to skillet and brown well on all sides. Add salt and chicken broth and simmer, covered, for 30 minutes until chicken is almost tender. Add papaya slices and simmer for 15 additional minutes until papaya is tender but not mushy. Remove chicken pieces to hot platter, spoon sauce and papaya slices over them and serve with rice. Serves 4.

CHICKEN IN LEMON-LIME JUICE

An easy to prepare marinade gives this chicken a tropical, tangy flavor. It's best if marinated overnight.

juice of 4 lemons
juice of 4 limes
1 clove garlic, minced
1 tsp. salt
2 tsp. dried tarragon leaves,
    crushed

1/2 tsp. white pepper
1 cup vegetable oil
1 cup dry white wine
2 chickens, 2-1/2 to 3 lbs. each,
    cut into serving pieces

Combine lemon and lime juice, garlic, salt, tarragon, pepper, oil and wine in large bowl. Stir to mix. Place chicken pieces in marinade. Cover tightly. Refrigerate at least 8 hours. Turn chicken pieces once while it marinates. Remove chicken from marinade. Place in shallow baking dish. Bake for 1 hour at 375°F., or until done. Baste once with marinade while cooking. Makes 6 to 8 servings.

Chicken Thighs with
◄ Sherry Stuffing (page 94)

Chicken With Fruit

CHICKEN IN PEACH SAUCE

2 tbs. vegetable oil
1/2 tsp. salt
1/2 tsp. pepper
1/4 tsp. paprika
1/2 tsp. poultry seasoning
1 chicken, 2-1/2 to 3 lbs.,
    cut into serving pieces

1/4 cup butter or margarine
1 cup finely chopped onion
5 tbs. lemon juice
4 large firm fresh peaches
1/2 cup sugar

Pour oil in large skillet. Place over medium-high heat. Sprinkle chicken with salt, pepper, paprika and poultry seasoning. Place chicken pieces in skillet and saute until brown on all sides. Add 1-1/4 cups water; simmer over low heat 25 minutes. Skim fat and discard. Melt 2 tablespoons butter in another skillet over medium heat and saute onion until golden. Remove onion from skillet. Pour one tablespoon lemon juice over onion and set aside. Wash, peel and slice peaches. Saute peach slices in remaining half of butter until golden. Mix together remaining lemon juice and sugar. Add onion, peaches, juice mixture and 3/4 cup water to chicken. Simmer, covered for 20 minutes. Makes 4 servings.

Chicken With Fruit

SAUCY CHICKEN WITH GRAPES

3 tbs. flour
1/2 tsp. salt
1/4 tsp. pepper
1 chicken, 3 lbs., cut into serving pieces
1/3 cup vegetable oil
3 tbs. honey

2 tbs. chopped parsley
3 tbs. grated orange rind
3/4 cup white wine
1/2 cup orange juice
1-1/4 cups seedless grapes

Mix flour, salt and pepper together in a shallow dish. Coat chicken pieces with flour mixture. Pour oil into large skillet. Place over medium-high heat. Add chicken to skillet and saute until brown on all sides. Add honey, parsley, orange rind, wine and juice. Cover and cook 40 minutes longer. Check chicken after it has cooked 20 minutes. If it seems dry, add 1/2 cup water. Remove chicken; skim and discard fat from sauce. Add grapes. Heat, pour sauce over chicken. Serve immediately. Makes 4 servings.

MOROCCAN-STYLE LEMON CHICKEN

1 lemon
1 chicken, 2-1/2 to 3 lbs.
   cut into serving pieces
salt and pepper
2 tbs. butter

2 shallots or scallions, finely chopped
1 clove garlic, minced
3/4 cup chicken stock
1/4 cup chopped fresh parsley
1 tsp. dried oregano

Cut rind of half the lemon into very thin strips. Reserve. Squeeze lemon. Reserve juice. Sprinkle chicken pieces with salt and pepper. Melt butter and oil in skillet over medium-high heat. Saute chicken until brown on all sides. Remove chicken from skillet. Add shallots and garlic to same skillet. Saute until golden. Add 1/4 cup of stock and stir to dissolve all brown particles clinging to bottom of skillet. Cook until liquid is almost evaporated. Add 1/2 cup more of stock. Reduce liquid, over medium heat, to 1/3 cup. Return chicken to skillet, sprinkle with parsley, oregano, lemon rind and juice. Cover and cook slowly, for about 40 minutes, or until chicken is done. Check chicken occasionally. If necessary, add up to 1 cup more chicken broth. Skim and discard fat before serving. Makes 4 servings.

PINEAPPLE CHICKEN

A tart and sweet taste from the Hawaiian Islands.

2 chickens, 2-1/2 to 3 lbs. each, quartered or halved
1/4 cup vegetable oil
salt and pepper
2 tbs. sugar
1 tsp. cornstarch
1 can (8-1/4 ozs.) crushed pineapple
2 tbs. butter or margarine
2 tbs. soy sauce
1 tbs. finely chopped onion

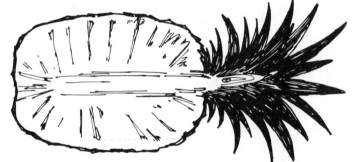

Break joints of chicken. Brush chicken all over with oil. Sprinkle with salt and pepper. Broil or barbecue 4 to 5 inches from heat, 15 to 20 minutes per side. Meanwhile, in small saucepan combine sugar, cornstarch, pineapple, butter, soy sauce and onion. Cook and stir until thickened and bubbly. Spoon mixture over chicken during last 5 minutes of broiling. Makes 6 to 8 servings.

Chicken With Fruit

NUTS AND SEEDS ACCOMPANY CHICKEN

ALMOND-ENCRUSTED CHICKEN

Crunchy almonds add interest to this simple dish. After you roll the chicken in almonds, this dish may be refrigerated for up to 24 hours.

1 egg
1/2 cup milk
1/2 tsp. salt
1 tsp. paprika
flour
1 chicken, 2-1/2 to 3 lbs., cut into serving pieces
1 cup sliced almonds
1/2 cup vegetable oil

Beat egg lightly with milk, salt and paprika. Dip chicken pieces, one at a time, into flour, then into egg mixture. Roll in almonds. Pour oil into shallow baking dish. Arrange chicken pieces in pan, skin side up. Bake at 375°F. for 1 to 1-1/2 hours, basting twice during baking process. Makes 4 servings.

With Nuts & Seeds

CHICKEN WITH WALNUTS

A quickly prepared chicken dish with lots of vegetables and nuts. Serve it with rice and a Mandarin orange salad.

2 tbs. cornstarch
1 tsp. sugar
1 tbs. soy sauce
1/4 cup vegetable oil
1/2 cup coarsely chopped walnuts
1 onion, sliced

1 sweet red pepper, seeded, deribbed and sliced
2 cups diced cooked chicken
1-1/2 cups chicken broth
2 tbs. sherry
3/4 cup chopped celery

Mix together cornstarch, sugar and soy sauce to make a smooth paste. Pour oil into wok or large skillet. Place over high heat. Saute walnuts, onion and pepper in oil 4 to 5 minutes. Add chicken and chicken broth. Stir. Blend in cornstarch paste and simmer 3 to 5 minutes, stirring constantly. Add sherry and celery and cook 2 minutes more. Serve immediately. Makes 4 servings.

CHICKEN WITH CASHEW NUTS

The flavors of chicken and cashew nuts harmonize especially well in this dish.

1 egg white
2 chicken breasts, skinned, boned and diced
1-1/2 tsp. soy sauce
2 tsp. sherry
1/2 tsp. sugar
1/2 tsp. sesame oil
2 tsp. cornstarch
3 tbs. vegetable oil
3/4 cup salted cashews

Beat egg white in large bowl until foamy. Add chicken, salt, soy sauce, sherry, sugar, sesame oil and cornstarch to egg white. Pour oil in wok or large skillet. Place over high heat. Stir fry about 2 minutes. Add cashews, mix well, and serve immediately. Makes 4 servings.

With Nuts & Seeds

CHICKEN BAKED IN TOMATO-ALMOND PUREE

1 chicken, 3 lbs.,
    cut into serving pieces
1 cup lime juice
1/2 tsp. salt
1 can (17 ozs.) tomatoes, drained
2 whole cloves
6 peppercorns

2 bay leaves
1/4 cup water
2 slices French bread,
    each 1-1/2 inches thick, cubed
1 cup blanched almonds
1/3 cup vegetable oil
tomato and avocado slices (optional)

Marinate chicken pieces in lime juice and 1 teaspoon salt for one hour. Combine tomatoes, cloves, peppercorns, bay leaves, water and 1/2 teaspoon salt in blender jar. Puree. Pour oil in skillet. Place over medium-high heat. Fry bread cubes in oil until golden, about 2 minutes on each side. Drain on paper towels. Add cubes to tomato mixture. Saute almonds in oil until golden. Add almonds to tomato mixture. Puree mixture until smooth. Spread 1/3 of puree mixture in shallow baking dish. Remove chicken from marinade and arrange in dish over puree mixture. Cover with remaining puree. Bake uncovered, at 350°F. until chicken is tender, about 45 minutes. Garnish with tomato and avocado slices, if desired. Makes 4 servings.

GALLINA EN PIPIAN

This thick nut sauce is marvelous on chicken. For a change, combine sauce and chicken and spoon mixture into hot flour tortillas. You may use leftover cooked chicken in this recipe, too.

1 large chicken, cut into serving pieces,
   or 2 cups cubed cooked chicken
salt and pepper
3 cups chicken broth
1 can (6 ozs.) green chilies, seeded

1/2 cup toasted, shelled pumpkin
   seeds **OR** sunflower seeds
1/2 cup **EACH** peanuts and corn nuts
2 cloves garlic, peeled
salt and pepper

Boil 1-1/2 quarts of water in large saucepan or Dutch oven. Add chicken, salt and pepper. Simmer for 1 hour, or until chicken is tender. Remove chicken from saucepan. Reserve broth. When chicken is cool, remove meat from bones and cut into small pieces. Combine chilies with 1 cup reserved chicken broth, corn nuts, pumpkin seeds, peanuts and garlic in a blender jar. Blend until smooth. Add remaining chicken broth to sauce. Cook 10 minutes, stirring occasionally. Spoon sauce over cooked chicken. Makes 4 to 6 servings.

With Nuts & Seeds

CIRCASSIAN CHICKEN

A famous chicken dish from Turkey which has a rich walnut-thickened sauce.

3 whole cloves

3 onions

1 chicken, 2-1/2 to 3 lbs., cut into serving pieces

3 stalks celery

1 bay leaf

1/2 tsp. salt

8 peppercorns

1-1/2 cups walnuts

1/2 cup soft bread crumbs

1 to 2 tbs. paprika

1/4 tsp. cayenne pepper

Boil 2 quarts water in Dutch oven or large saucepan. Stick a clove into each onion. Add chicken, onions, celery, bay leaf, salt and peppercorns to water. Simmer 1 to 1-1/2 hours, or until chicken is tender. Remove chicken. By boiling, uncovered, reduce stock to one half its original volume. Strain and cool to lukewarm. Puree walnuts in blender jar. Add bread crumbs, 2 tablespoons reduced stock, paprika and cayenne. Blend again. Slowly add about 2 cups of lukewarm stock. Blend briefly until mixture has consistency of thin mayonnaise. Skin and bone chicken. Cut meat into bite-sized pieces. Spoon sauce over chicken and serve. Makes 4 servings.

CREATIVE WAYS WITH LEFTOVER CHICKEN

Creative Leftovers

EASY CHICKEN POT PIE

Don't let the reputation of frozen chicken pot pies stop you from trying this great casserole. This is so much better than its frozen "cousin" you won't believe they are related.

3 tbs. butter or margarine
1/2 cup chopped onion
1/4 cup all-purpose flour
1/2 tsp. salt
1/8 tsp. freshly ground pepper
1/2 tsp. poultry seasoning

2 cups chicken broth
2 cups cooked, chopped chicken
1 cup frozen peas and carrots, cooked
   and drained
4 refrigerated, unbaked biscuits

Melt butter in skillet over medium heat. Saute onion in butter 8 to 10 minutes, stirring constantly. Blend in flour, salt, pepper and poultry seasoning. Gradually add broth. Stir constantly while mixture thickens. Add chicken, peas and carrots. Heat until boiling. Pour into 1-1/2-quart casserole dish. Slice biscuits into quarters. Place on top of chicken mixture. Bake at 450°F. for 8 to 10 minutes, until biscuits are browned and done. Makes 4 servings.

CHICKEN-DRESSING BAKE

You don't have to go to the trouble of preparing stuffed roast chicken to enjoy chicken and dressing. Try this easy and colorful dish.

1 pkg. (8 ozs.) herb-seasoned stuffing mix
1 can (10-1/2 ozs.) cream of mushroom soup
2 cups chicken stock
2 well-beaten eggs
2-1/2 cups diced, cooked chicken
1/2 cup milk
2 tbs. chopped canned pimiento

Toss stuffing mix with 1/2 can of soup, 2 cups stock and eggs. Spread mixture in shallow baking dish. Top with chicken. Mix together milk, pimiento and remaining soup. Pour over chicken-dressing mixture. Cover with foil. Bake at 350°F. for 45 minutes. Makes 4 to 6 servings.

Creative Leftovers

CHICKEN AU GRATIN

Serve with crusty French bread and a fresh green salad.

1/4 cup butter or margarine
1/4 cup all-purpose flour
1 tsp. salt
1/2 tsp. pepper
2 cups milk
1/2 cup shredded sharp cheddar cheese
4 cups chopped cooked chicken
1/2 cup bread crumbs

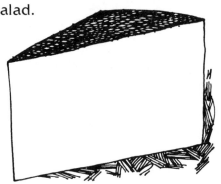

Melt butter in large skillet over medium heat. Add flour, salt and pepper. Cook, stirring constantly, for about 7 to 8 minutes. Gradually add milk. Cook, stirring constantly until sauce is thick and smooth. Add cheese. Continue cooking and stirring until melted. Remove skillet from heat. Place chicken in buttered casserole and pour cheese sauce on top. Sprinkle with bread crumbs. Bake at 350°F. for 35 to 40 minutes. Makes 4 to 6 servings.

140   Chicken-Vegetable Casserole (page 54) ▶

ALMOND CHICKEN CASSEROLE

This recipe is easy enough to prepare any day of the week. The real bonus is that it's also delicious enough to serve to your most special company.

1/2 cup sliced fresh mushrooms
1 tbs. butter
3 cups cooked rice
1 cup chicken broth
3 cups cubed cooked chicken
3/4 cup chopped celery
1 can (10-1/2 ozs.) cream of mushroom soup
1 cup sliced almonds

Saute mushrooms in butter just until limp. Combine mushrooms, rice, chicken broth, chicken, celery and soup. Pour into greased 1-quart casserole dish. Sprinkle with almonds. Bake at 325°F. for 45 minutes. Makes 4 to 6 servings.

◀ Easy Chicken Pot Pie (page 138)   **141**

CHICKEN-TANGERINE STUFFED CREPES

The next two recipes present delicious ways to prepare leftover chicken in crepes. An easy and foolproof recipe for crepes precedes the filling recipes.

CREPES

6 tbs. butter

2 eggs

1/4 cup milk

1/4 cup water

1 tbs. brandy (optional)

1/2 cup all-purpose flour

1/4 tsp. salt

Have ready a small frying pan or skillet (bottom measurement of 6 to 8 inches) or crepe pan, a blender or electric beater, small spatula and a warm plate. In skillet, melt butter until foaming over medium heat. Skim and discard foam. Carefully pour out clear amber liquid butter, discarding milky residue. This is called "clarified" butter. Use clarified butter in recipe and for cooking crepes. Combine eggs, milk, water, brandy, 1 tablespoon clarified butter, flour and salt in blender jar. Blend until smooth. Let batter stand at room temperature 1 hour. When ready to cook, heat small skillet until quite hot. Add 1/2 teaspoon clarified butter and about 2 tablespoons batter. Rotate pan so a thin film of batter forms on bottom. Work quickly, crepe will be ready to turn in 15 to 20 seconds. When crepe has browned on one side, use spatula to flip over. Let opposite side cook 15 seconds. Slide onto warmed plate. Repeat procedure, buttering pan before each crepe. Makes 12 to 16 crepes.

CHICKEN TANGERINE STUFFING

1 can (6 ozs.) water chestnuts, drained and sliced
1 can (8 ozs.) tangerines, drained
2 cups diced, cooked chicken
1/2 cup **EACH** mayonnaise and chopped almonds
2 tbs. sherry

1/4 tsp. salt
SAUCE
1/2 cup mayonnaise
1/2 cup sour cream

Combine water chestnuts, tangerines, chicken, mayonnaise, almonds, sherry and salt. Mix gently, but thoroughly. Place 2 tablespoons mixture on each crepe and fold sides together. Place rolled crepes into greased baking dish. Combine all sauce ingredients. Pour over crepes. Bake at 325°F. for 30 minutes. Makes 4 to 6 servings.

CHICKEN PRALINE CREPES

A rich, prize winning recipe. Use the crepe recipe on page 142.

CREPE FILLING
2 cups diced, cooked chicken
3/4 cup slivered almonds
3/4 cup halved pecans
1 tbs. minced watercress
1/2 cup sour cream
1/2 tsp. **EACH** salt and white pepper
12 crepes (see recipe, page 142)

BRANDIED CHERRY SAUCE
1 can (9-1/2 ozs.) dark, sweet cherries, pitted
1/4 cup firmly packed brown sugar
1/2 cup apricot brandy
2 tbs. cornstarch

Mix together chicken, almonds, pecans, watercress, sour cream, salt and pepper. Spoon filling into crepes, fold sides together. Line bottom of greased shallow baking dish with folded crepes. Bake at 300°F. for 20 minutes. Prepare sauce. Heat cherries and syrup in small saucepan 5 minutes. Add sugar and brandy. Stir until sugar dissolves. Add cornstarch and cook until thickened. Pour sauce over cooked crepes. Makes 4 to 6 servings.

CHICKEN TETRAZZINI

This dish was invented in honor of an opera star, and bears her name.

1/4 cup butter or margarine
3/4 lb. mushrooms, sliced
1 green pepper, slivered
3 tbs. all-purpose flour
1-1/2 tsp. salt
1/4 tsp. pepper
2-1/2 cups half and half (light cream)

4 cups diced, cooked chicken
1/4 cup sherry
1/4 tsp. Tabasco sauce
6 ozs. uncooked spaghetti
2 egg yolks, beaten
2 tbs. grated Parmesan cheese

Melt butter in skillet over medium heat. Saute mushrooms and pepper 5 minutes. Blend in flour, salt and pepper. Add cream, stirring constantly. Cook until thickened. Add chicken and sherry, and heat. Season with Tabasco sauce. Cook spaghetti according to package directions. Drain spaghetti and pour into shallow greased baking dish. Add small amount of chicken mixture to egg yolks, then stir yolks into remaining chicken mixture. Pour over spaghetti. Sprinkle with cheese. Bake at 300°F. for 45 minutes. Makes 6 servings.

Creative Leftovers

CHICKEN AND SWEET POTATO PIE

You'll be reminded of Thanksgiving when you sample this spicy dish. This is sure to be a hit with pumpkin pie lovers.

2 cups mashed sweet potatoes
2 tbs. firmly packed brown sugar
1/4 tsp. salt
1/2 tsp. cinnamon
1/8 tsp. allspice
1/3 cup undiluted evaporated milk

2 tbs. butter
1/4 cup finely minced onions
1 can (5 ozs.) water chestnuts, quartered
1 can (10-1/2 ozs.) cream of chicken soup
3 cups cooked, diced chicken

Mix sweet potatoes, brown sugar, salt, cinnamon, allspice and milk together in bowl. Spread mixture in a ring in a greased 2-quart casserole dish. In a skillet, melt butter over medium heat. Saute onions and water chestnuts about 5 minutes, or until onions are translucent. Add soup, chicken and 2 tablespoons water. Heat, stirring occasionally. Pour into center of potato-ringed casserole. Bake at 400°F. for 20 to 30 minutes. Makes 6 servings.

SAVORY CHICKEN SALAD

Serve on a bed of lettuce, in tomato cups, avocado shells or melon halves. For variety add one cup seedless grape halves.

2 cups diced, cooked chicken
1 cup diced celery
1/4 tsp. salt
1/4 tsp. pepper
1/2 cup broken pecans or slivered almonds
1/2 cup mayonnaise or salad dressing
lettuce leaves
wedges of hard-cooked eggs, pickles, pickled beets, radishes, tomato wedges,
    sliced cucumber and olives for garnish (all optional)

Mix together chicken, celery, salt, pepper, nuts and mayonnaise. Serve on salad greens, adding optional ingredients as garnishes.

Creative Leftovers

SPECIAL CHICKEN PARTS

RUMAKI

A sophisticated Island favorite that is a popular appetizer on the Mainland as well.

1 doz. large chicken livers, intact
1 can (6 ozs.) drained water chestnuts
12 slices smoked bacon
1 cup soy sauce
6 tsp. dry sherry
2 cloves garlic, minced
1/2 tsp. ginger juice or minced fresh ginger

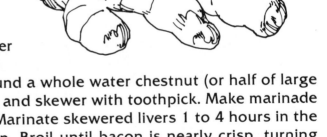

Cut the livers in half. Wrap liver around a whole water chestnut (or half of large one). Wrap 1/2-slice bacon around both, and skewer with toothpick. Make marinade of soy sauce, sherry, garlic, and ginger. Marinate skewered livers 1 to 4 hours in the refrigerator, turning once or twice. Drain. Broil until bacon is nearly crisp, turning once. Makes 6 to 8 appetizer servings.

Special Chicken Parts

CHICKEN GIZZARDS, SAUCE PIETRO

1/4 lb. bacon, finely chopped
1 tbs. olive oil
1 small onion, minced
2 garlic cloves, minced
1 lb. chicken gizzards, chopped
2 parsley sprigs, minced
1/4 to 1/2 tsp. crushed red pepper
1/4 tsp. ground cloves

1/2 tsp. crumbled dried marjoram
1/4 tsp. salt
1 cup dry red wine
2 cups fresh or canned, chopped tomatoes
2 cans (6 ozs. each) tomato paste
4 cups water
8 ozs. thin spaghetti
grated Romano or Parmesan cheese

Cook bacon, olive oil, onion and garlic in large saucepan over medium heat until bacon is nearly crisp. Add gizzards, parsley, red pepper, cloves, marjoram and salt. Cook 2 to 3 minutes. Add wine. Simmer, covered for about 25 minutes. Add tomatoes, tomato paste and water. Simmer until fairly thick. Cook spaghetti according to package directions and drain. Sprinkle platter with cheese. Add spaghetti to platter, cover with sauce and sprinkle with more cheese. Makes 6 servings.

CHICKEN LIVERS IN PORT WINE

A savory favorite, equally suited for chafing dish or stove top cooking.

1/3 cup butter or margarine
4 green onions, finely chopped
1 lb. chicken livers
1/4 tsp. dried sage
1/4 tsp. salt
2 tbs. lemon juice
2/3 cup Port wine
1/4 tsp. freshly ground pepper
slices of toast

Melt butter in skillet over medium heat. Saute onions in butter for 8 to 10 minutes. Add livers, saute 4 minutes. Stir in sage, salt, lemon juice, Port and pepper. Simmer about 8 minutes, stirring occasionally. Correct seasonings and serve on toast. Makes 3 to 4 servings.

Special Chicken Parts

CHICKEN WINGS, PARMESAN

Chicken wings have become fashionable and popular as appetizers.

2 to 2-1/2 lbs. chicken wings
1/3 cup butter or margarine, melted
2/3 cup all-purpose flour
1/2 tsp. salt
1/3 cup grated Parmesan cheese
1/2 tsp. paprika
1/2 tsp. oregano
1/2 cup buttermilk

Cut off tips of wings. Discard or save in freezer for chicken broth. Pour butter into foil-lined shallow baking dish. Preheat oven to 400°F. Mix flour, salt, cheese, paprika, and oregano together in a bowl. Dip wings in buttermilk, roll in flour-cheese mixture, then in melted butter. Bake in foil-lined dish 1 hour, or until crisp. Makes 4 servings as main dish, or 6 to 8 servings as appetizer.

SPICY CHINESE CHICKEN WINGS

Hoisin sauce has a sweet and pungent flavor. It's available in the Oriental sections of most supermarkets.

1/4 cup sesame oil
1/2 cup soy sauce
1/4 cup honey
2 green onions, chopped
1 tsp. garlic powder
3 tbs. Hoisin sauce
2 to 3 lbs. chicken wings (tips removed and discarded), cut into 2 pieces each

Mix sesame oil, soy sauce, honey, onions, garlic powder and Hoisin sauce together in a shallow glass dish. Add wings and marinate 4 to 6 hours in the refrigerator. Place in shallow baking dish and bake at 350°F. for 30 minutes. Remove from oven and cool. Just before serving broil 5 minutes to brown. Watch carefully during broiling to keep wings from charing. Makes 6 to 8 appetizer servings.

Special Chicken Parts

INDEX

Index